From
This Day Forward

From This

Staying Married When No One Else Is and Other Reckless Acts

Day Forward

LOUISE DeGRAVE

LITTLE, BROWN AND COMPANY   BOSTON / TORONTO

FIRST EDITION

Portions of this book have appeared in slightly different form in
the *Los Angeles Times* and the *La Jolla Light*. An excerpt has
appeared in *McCall's*.

LIBRARY OF CONGRESS CATALOGING IN PUBLICATION DATA
DeGrave, Louise.
From this day forward.
1. Marriage—United States—Anecdotes, facetiae,
satire, etc. 2. Family—United States—Anecdotes,
facetiae, satire, etc. 3. Housewives—United
States—Anecdotes, facetiae, satire, etc. I. Title.
HQ536.D36   306.8   80-206
ISBN 0-316-17930-2   AACR2

BC
Designed by Susan Windheim.
Published simultaneously in Canada
by Little, Brown & Company (Canada) Limited
PRINTED IN THE UNITED STATES OF AMERICA

for Margaret Smith Dursin

Acknowledgments

I'd like to thank:

Isaac and Pauline, who gave me such wonderful material to write about

Gilbert Moore, for giving me a chance

Carol Noland, who has been a second mother to my children

Philippa Brophy, for persevering

Mary Tondorf-Dick, who has a great future in diplomacy if she ever gives up editing

Trish Stanley, because she cares

And the friends who said, "Don't give up. It'll fly."

Contents

Introduction
Personality Styles

Issues of Early Marriage

Problems of Everyday Living

Family Planning, Part 1: Adoption

Marriage and the Modern Woman

Dealing with the World around You

Family Planning, Part 2: Birth

After the Early Years

Epilogue

Introduction

"*P*urposes of marriage: *A universal biopsychosocial need for completion and fulfillment of oneself through the intimate life with another exists among humans and some other species . . . In the West, partners choose each other by and large on the basis of their feelings and hopes, be they realistic or not. Among the less conscious motivations and unrealistic factors that lead to marriage are many neurotic tendencies and needs . . .*

"Not all unconscious or external determinants need be unsound. The choice of a marital partner is a complex process, and a certain intuitive sense of personality fit between two people seems to operate effectively at times, even if neither spouse can account for it explicitly. There are many paths to marriage, sound and unsound foundations for family life, but spouses can build sound relationships even if they have united for ill considered reasons. One of the chief criteria for a successful marriage is that it furthers individual growth and growth as a unit . . .

"The personalities and the sociocultural values two individuals bring to marriage determine the nature of their relationship more than do their hopes, dreams, and intentions during courtship."

—A. M. Freedman and H. I. Kaplan, eds.
Comprehensive Textbook of Psychiatry

I learned a long time ago that marriage gives you not so much a helpmate as a scapegoat.

Actually, I got my first exposure to this concept before I even married Ralph, but I was too enamored of his handsome body, quick mind, and potential earning power to pay attention.

During our engagement, I should explain, Ralph was living in a dormitory on a sub-subsistence budget, and one of the ways he economized was to do all of his laundry — darks, whites, and in-betweens — in one load. Part of the problem was, of course, that even standing on the machine lid, it's tough to get a month's laundry into one small machine.

"Ralph," I said at the time, "there is no room in there for the water. And the stuff that is sticking out of the top is not going to get clean."

"Nonsense," said Ralph, the perennial optimist. "As soon as the lower stuff gets wet, it'll sink down, and with a little brute force . . ." I'm sure the owner of those machines still has a warrant out for Ralph's arrest.

"Now, for the soap," said Ralph, unhooking a dispenser of that green liquid goop that was hanging on the wall next to the sink and pouring it in. (I mean, that stuff wasn't even any good on *hands*.)

Every month, Ralph's wardrobe descended into deeper shades of gray until he heard about an inexpensive laundry nearby where a little old man would run your clothes through the machine for you and even fold them up afterward. (Ralph was never much on folding.) He decided to try it.

When the little old man dumped out Ralph's clothes on the counter, his face registered disbelief. "*Who* used to do your laundry?" he said finally.

Ralph didn't bat an eyelash. "She did," he said, pointing to me.

The next day, when we went back to pick it up, the little old man shook his head at Ralph. "If you haven't married this girl yet, I wouldn't," he said. "It took me three washes to get it clean and, in the process, all the staples fell out. Did you know that's how she mends your clothes?"

"*Staples?*" I said. I really couldn't believe it.

"Fortunately, she has a nice personality," said Ralph.

When yet another of our friends announced not long ago that she was getting a divorce, Ralph and I had to ask ourselves, "Is there something wrong with us that we're still married?" Really. Are we still together simply because we are too insecure, weak of ego, or frightened of change to make it on our respective own? Is divorce a necessary rite of passage for growth? Is there such a thing as a healthy marriage?

These are sticky issues and I go back and forth on them. "Forth" whenever we see a certain couple we know who do seem to have a good marriage, and "back" whenever my twice-divorced friend Martha greets me with, "Hi, Louise. How's slavery?"

Now, Ralph and I have no plans to get a divorce, but I certainly can't say it will never happen. Some morning, I might wake up and look at Ralph's clothes hanging in their customary place over the curtain rod and something in me will snap. (I think this is what's known as an irreconcilable difference.)

And heaven knows, if we want a divorce, we have grounds.

In my petition, I would probably name the time during our courtship when Ralph took me to the local stables and told me not to tell them I didn't know how to ride or they would give me a really slow horse. Only because I was nineteen and an idiot did I agree.

I won't even go into the whole story about how the horse immediately tore off across the field and how I lost the reins and the stirrups and had my arms wrapped around the beast's neck, hanging on for dear life as I'm bouncing wildly up and down, and about Ralph galloping along behind yelling, "You're doing great! Sit up a little straighter!"

If I had to cite additional grounds, I'd probably name our moving night in Colorado, the one where we had only seven hours to move from one furnished rental house to another, and Ralph accepted a band job for six and a half of them. That, however, I could have forgiven him for. What I couldn't forgive him for was not telling me he had availed himself of Safeway's special that week and bought fifteen ten-pound bags of kitty litter, neatly stacked in the hall closet, which I ended up hauling out to the car, a bag at a time, in sub-zero weather at two o'clock in the morning. For that, I think I deserve both the house *and* the car.

Of course, Ralph has a few grounds against me too. However, no matter what he tells people, I did not *intentionally* pour the pot of boiling oil on his newly planted ivy. There were mitigating circumstances.

Certainly the last ten years have not always been easy. (That may be the biggest understatement I ever make.) We've had some pretty dramatic problems: the burglaries and the fire and the infertility and all. Combine those with two very young people from very different backgrounds who don't know each other as well as they think; a limited income; two less-than-perfect personalities; a lot of hopes and dreams and good intentions — and I guess you have Ralph and me. Making life hard.

What it all comes down to — this whole issue about marriage and divorce — is that, whichever state you're in, you like to think you're making the healthiest choice for yourself. And that whatever's right for you ought to be right for a lot of other people too. Maybe that's why married people and divorced people make each other feel a little defensive sometimes.

For example, I remember the night when Martha came over and introduced us to her new resident boyfriend.

"We have no need for marriage," Martha insisted. "We have a mature relationship based on mutual respect and love. We come home at night because we *feel* like it, not because we have to. We are faithful to each other because we *choose* to, not because of some stupid piece of paper that practically sentences you to a life of stifling monotony, compulsory togetherness, infantile overdependence, and boring sex, gradually strangling what tiny fragments remain of the beautiful feelings two human beings once had for each other and frequently leading both partners to alcoholism, drug abuse, mental illness, and emotional degradation, not to mention — "

"I think I'm getting depressed," I said.

"See?" said Martha. "That's just what marriage does to you!"

I guess the reason I'm thinking about marriage a lot is that last week was our tenth anniversary.

Coincidentally, the day before, I happened to find the packet of love letters I wrote to Ralph during our courtship. Absence may make the heart grow fonder. But it also makes the brain grow mushy.

The letters were all written to an individual referred to as "Lambie," whose name was invariably preceded by a long list of adoring adjectives. The margins were elaborately decorated with arrow-struck hearts, flowers, musical notes, soaring birds, sad faces, assorted stick figures acting out scenes of future domestic bliss, poetic verse, several hundred Xs labeled "kisses," and all manner of optimistic postscripts, including, "I cannot imagine ever having another unhappy moment after we are married."

As far as the actual contents were concerned, Ralph's mother once found some of my letters to him and pronounced them "revolting." Infatuation may not inspire great prose in the nineteen-year-old mind, but you have to love the enthusiasm. (The medium and the margins were the message.)

I'd almost forgotten, by the way, that I used to call Ralph a lamb. My younger sister Marie and I were engaged at the same time, and she referred to her intended as either a "cuddly bunny" or a "woolly bear."

"Sounds like a goddam zoo around here," my father used to mutter when both swains were in residence. For her side, Mother admitted several years ago that she nearly got sick every time she overheard Ralph saying goodnight to me, although my personal recollection was that he was terribly eloquent.

At the time, neither my sister nor I could understand why the folks were so upset by our persistent use of animal similes. Heck, we pointed out, even the Marine Corps used them. ("OK, you maggots, fall in.")

I can't remember now exactly when my husband made the metamorphosis from sheepdom to Ralphness. But I suspect it was somewhere around the day he lost his car keys for the fifty-seventh time.

I also keep thinking about a letter to Ann Landers from a woman who was mad at her husband because he kept leaving the toilet seat up, and their five-year-old was always forgetting to look first and kept falling in. Once upon a time, before the kids and the mortgage and the reality set in, she was probably nineteen and wrote gushy letters to the guy. Now she writes letters to Ann Landers about toilet seats.

There are some things in life that are just too cruel.

Personality Styles

(Or, You have your M.O. and I have my M.O.,
and if we should happen to marry, it's chaos)

A personality style implies a repetitive mode of response that is based on lifelong experience. Over the course of an individual's life, a coping style gradually evolves from a variety of positive and negative determinants, including family expectations, reactions to the parents' own characterological styles, major life events, constitutional factors, and compensations for real or perceived deficiencies. After marriage, couples may find that their individual coping styles are in themselves an area of conflict that exacerbate problems that could have relatively simple solutions. It is thus of some importance that marriage partners develop the ability to differentiate between the actual merits of an issue that needs to be resolved, their individual personality responses to it, and the dynamics of their interaction as a couple.

This is easier said than done.

The confidence game

Everybody has his forbidden fantasies. Mine is walking into a bookstore and buying a copy of Donny and Marie's fan magazine.

From time to time I take a peek at one, first looking furtively around to make sure no one is watching. But rather than sate my appetite, this only whets it more.

Of course, there's no point in buying one, because I could

never bring it home. What if I were hit by a truck the next day and Ralph and my relatives found it among my belongings?

Some day, of course, I plan to write about this and other trials in my memoirs, entitled *Confessions of a Closet Shlock Artist*, to be published only in a foreign language and under a pseudonym. In it, I will bare the deepest secrets of my soul; for example, that I prefer the *Ladies' Home Journal* to *Harper's*, have never gotten past page three of a Faulkner novel, and thought *Last Year at Marienbad* was the most boring movie I ever saw.

Now, every forbidden fantasy is rooted somewhere, usually in some deep trauma of one's formative years. Mine, I think, stems from the fact that for the majority of my life, I have been surrounded by people of genuine cultural merit. People who actually read the *Saturday Review* because they liked it, not because they thought suffering builds character.

My parents, I should mention, met in an honors Shakespeare class at Brown University. My brother and sister both had a genius for SATs and National Merit Exams. All four of them were repositories of vast quantities of esoteric information, the result of being rapid and voracious readers. I read too, but slowly, and with my lips until I was twenty-three.

They weren't snobs about it or anything. But since I was nine years old, a burning question has lurked in the back of my mind: Would they love me if they knew I was a wasteland?

Never one to leave bad enough alone, I went and married Ralph, who came with a Phi Beta Kappa key, a physics prize, and an extensive knowledge of classical music.

You could sum up the difference between Ralph and me in that I secretly like Debbie Boone's singing of "You Light Up My Life." Ralph regards it as a felony.

So I ask you, is this a household where you could watch Donny and Marie, much less buy their fan magazine?

As may be obvious by now, a lot of my problems have to do with confidence.

I guess it all started back in elementary school when the guidance counselor used to tell my mother that my brother, Pierre (a year older), and my sister, Marie (a year younger), were little geniuses.

"What about Louise?" said Mother.

"Well . . . she *tries* hard . . ."

Louise, alas, has had a long and uncontested career as the family idiot.

Since I was a blue-eyed blond in a family of brown-eyed brunettes, you couldn't help but wonder if the babies had been switched in the hospital. Somewhere in the greater Boston area was a family of blond dum-dums who inexplicably ended up with a brunette genius.

Oh, the family tried hard to make me feel at home by passing me off as a "recessive" (which for years I confused with "regressive") or trying to find some remote family resemblance ("She has Aunt Harriet's fanny").

And it wasn't as though they never praised me. I remember once when our dog, Josephine Bonaparte, was misbehaving and I said, "Josephine, you are a recalcitrant animal!" Recalcitrant being one of the words I had to memorize for a vocabulary test that week. The whole family looked up from their books.

"Louise used a big word," said Pierre.

"Way to go, Louise," said Marie.

Being a cretin, I knew I had to work much harder in school than most people. My junior-high-school guidance counselor told me that I was an "overachiever."

"What's that?" I said.

"That's a person who achieves more than he is capable of," she explained. I never could figure out how that could be, but only took that as further evidence of my mental insufficiencies. I did finally ask her, however, how they knew what I was capable of.

"From your aptitude tests," she said. "We all have our special gifts, and yours just happen to be different from Pierre's and Marie's. You did *very* well in mathematics and mechanics." She thought I was a natural for building construction.

What's always confused me is that, despite my terrific mechanical aptitude, I can't even oil the electric can opener successfully. On the aptitude test, all I had to do was figure out which way Wheel A would turn if Wheel G were rotated counterclockwise. A cinch.

For years I had this fantasy that some desperate person would come rushing up to me on the street and say, "I've got this life-or-death problem with these interconnecting wheels," and I would confidently say, "Leave it to me," and achieve national fame.

By the time I was in high school, I had really developed a complex about all this. (It seemed the only sane thing to do.) Face it, if you have a brother and sister who learn by osmosis and you don't, in a house where educational achievement matters, you have two choices. You place yourself in foster care, or you work hard and get very organized. I chose the latter.

Now, all the world may love a lover, but nobody loves an organized person.

Really. Organized people are among the most discriminated against on the face of the earth.

The ironic part about it is that on New Year's Eve, about half the population of this country resolves that this year, they're "going to get organized." You'd think it was a desirable trait. I guess it's sort of like virginity. You're supposed to aspire to it, but if you've got it, nobody admires you for it.

Comedians, columnists, and cartoonists love to make fun of organized people.

Psychologists intimate that we had overly strict toilet training and that we stay up nights playing with our collections of string and aluminum-foil scraps.

Your friends will forgive you many things — cattiness, sloth, a live-in babysitter — but not being organized.

Actually, I can say with some authority that it is very rare for a child to survive to adulthood being organized. It was not, as I personally discovered, a trait that our educational system rewarded, despite pretensions to the contrary.

I got my first real lesson in this in the seventh grade when our social-studies teacher, Mr. Ash, assigned everybody in the class to write a report about the Algonquin Indians, to be due in five days. I diligently researched it the first day, wrote it the second, copied it over the third, only to have it canceled on the fourth, on the grounds that "nobody" had started it anyway.

Let me just say that there is nothing more useless than a leftover report on the Algonquin Indians, except maybe a report on the insect of one's choice or a term paper on "Symbolism in *The Scarlet Letter*," last-minute cancellations in the eighth and tenth grades, respectively.

It never ceased to amaze me throughout high school and college how teachers would exhort us not to leave a forty-page term paper for the last minute, but then waited until the last week to decide on the format — or, more often than not, to suddenly succumb to pressure and make the project "optional."

I may have been organized, but I did have my self-respect, and no kid with even half his marbles would have dreamed of doing an optional project knowing ahead of time it was optional. But there I'd be, stuck with some dog like "The effect of meaningfulness and syntax on free-recall learning," and what was I going to do with it?

I can't describe the loss of peer respect I suffered handing in an "optional" term paper on the last day of class. Whenever possible, I tried to sneak it in early and leave it on the teacher's desk in a plain brown wrapper, but inevitably some malicious procrastinator saw me and told the whole class.

In college, I simply went underground. I organized some

very effective ways to look disorganized, like leaving my lights on all night before an exam so no one would know I'd already studied. I became a closet organized person.

The point I started out to make with all this is that even though I compensated for my lack of confidence by being organized and doing well in school, it didn't solve my basic problem: Someday, someone was going to figure out I was playing out of my league. In the midst of all this, I got married.

Frankly, my lack of confidence has really caused some problems between Ralph and me. In the beginning of our marriage especially, I just couldn't seem to deal with people having expectations of me. This drove Ralph crazy.

I hate to admit it, but I have always done well in jobs where I initially led my employer to believe I had an IQ of twenty-eight and suffered from dyslexia. Then I could relax and do an astounding job, and my bosses would be surprised and delighted that the new employee could not only type but also write and do a little translating as well, and everybody would be wildly happy until they'd go and ruin it all by wanting to promote me.

After a while, I learned to screen my jobs more carefully.

"What are my chances for promotion?" I'd inquire.

"Excellent," my prospective boss would say with a smile.

"No, thank you," I'd say.

So everything was going along beautifully and I was having a wildly successful career being unsuccessful. I had a wonderful job that paid adequately with no chance of advancement in sight. But then I got an offer of a job that paid much better.

Now, I have always had a lot of trouble explaining to people why I might be averse to being paid well, especially to my husband, Ralph.

"You turned down the job because the salary was too good?" he screamed with great gnashing of teeth and tearing out of hair. (Ralph has always been high-strung.)

As I explained to him, when the salary is low, you can reasonably control expectations. Let's say your boss doesn't like your work. If he's paying you well, he says, "This is what I'm paying you all that money for, to produce this crappola?" And he makes you feel anxious and terrible and implies that if you don't do better you'll be fired, so you slither home and develop high blood pressure and an ulcer worrying about the humiliation of having failed and about the gifts that the kids (if you had any) wouldn't be getting this Christmas, not to mention you'll probably lose everything and have to go on welfare, and God knows nobody loves a loser.

But if you're not being paid well, you could look the boss right in the eye and say, "So what do you want for four twenty-five an hour? Simone de Beauvoir?" And you tell him if he gives you any more flak you'll quit and go somewhere else (where they also pay four twenty-five an hour), which he doesn't want you to do because as long as you're feeling independent and confident, you're producing this terrific stuff.

Now, let me be the first to say that over the past ten years, I've improved immeasurably on this, and my head understands that you have to learn to deal with high expectations and risk failure and seek a salary commensurate with your abilities.

My stomach, however, still likes it the other way.

Sloth be not proud

Ralph, of course, has his little quirks too. Maybe I shouldn't say this in print, but I married one of the biggest slobs in the Western Hemisphere.

In his defense, I'd like to say that he's a selective slob. I'd eat off the floor of his toolshed. He always looks well-groomed and his office is a paragon of efficiency.

His home, however, looks like Nicaragua after the earthquake.

The amazing thing about it is that when Ralph and I were engaged, I was really impressed at how deeply he seemed to believe in women's rights. Here was a man who stated unequivocally that housework was not just "women's work."

What I didn't find out until later was that he believed just as deeply that it was not "Ralph work" either.

Actually, Ralph has never perceived housework to be much of a problem. From his experience, dirt is something that if left long enough will simply go away. The concept that he has never grasped is that a female human being had some part in this.

I remember when we first got married, Ralph would be making himself a bedtime snack and drop plunks of tomato sauce all across the kitchen floor, which he somehow never seemed to notice.

The first 650 times, of course, I grabbed a sponge and, as all brides are wont to do in their Predisillusionment Phase, cheerfully cleaned it up. But after a while, it got me kind of annoyed.

"Hey!" I said one night, when the Midnight Chef had let a whole pan of soup boil over on the stove. "Just who do you think is going to clean this up, anyway?" The soup, charred on the burner, had overflowed the stove top and run down the oven door, forming a little pool on the floor.

Ralph looked up from the kitchen table where he was quietly enjoying his repast and gazed quizzically at the mess on the stove as though he'd never seen it before. A faintly troubled look came across his face as if a new and foreign concept were entering his mind for the first time.

"Just who's going to clean this up?" I demanded again, meanwhile cleaning it up. At that stage, I was still worried he wouldn't love me if I didn't. Later on, I *knew* he wouldn't, but it didn't bother me as much.

All Ralph knew was that up to this point in his life, whoever cleaned things up hadn't been him. There was no malice toward me or conscious oppression intended in his leaving a mess in the kitchen. He simply hadn't been trained to notice it. (I suspect he also realized on some level that it behooved him not to start.)

There was a lot of tomato sauce under the sponge before I finally realized that Ralph's liberal theories about housework bore no resemblance to his practice. In Ralph's defense, however, I will say that this was not entirely his fault.

Ralph and his two brothers (no sisters) grew up in a house where dirt, spills, and wet towels on the bathroom floor disappeared like magic. Never a nag about hanging up clothes; never a harsh word about tomato sauce on the kitchen floor. Ralph's mother, alas, was your archetypal doormat.

She always told the boys not to waste their time in mundane household chores; they should instead study and make something of themselves. If I had my way, it would be a felony for a mother to do that. She would be tried by a jury of her daughter-in-law's peers, and believe me, she wouldn't stand a chance.

Actually, I have a lot of sympathy for Ralph's mother. It could not have been easy living with a man who believes in the innate inferiority of women as much as Ralph's father does. Poor Mom was just trying to be a dedicated wife and mother. (And she certainly was.)

Now, every housewife has blind spots — dirty spots in her home that she doesn't see even though she lives there and looks right at them all the time. The upshot of Mom's efforts was that she produced three sons for whom the entire interior of their homes was a blind spot. For the sons' brides, this was a devastating revelation.

Frankly, this was really driving me up the wall, and after a lot of nagging about it, I finally decided to ask our good friend Greg, a psychologist, for his advice about a problem a "friend" of mine was having.

"It all started," I said, "when my friend met this guy when

she was in college. She was so in love with him that she almost didn't notice that the guy and his roommate hadn't cleaned their bathroom once during the whole year. But she's young and adaptable, so she wore beach thongs in the shower, operated the sink faucets with a pair of pliers, and the toilet I won't go into.

"Well, they planned to get married the fall after he graduated. So the night before he has to be out of his apartment in the spring, she comes over and notices that he hasn't even started to pack, not to mention there are six weeks' worth of dirty dishes and pots in the sink, and she gets all excited and says, 'How are you possibly going to be out of here by tomorrow?' And he tells her not to worry.

"And sure enough, when she comes back the next morning, everything's all packed up. And she says, 'I can't believe you washed all those dishes and packed everything up in such a short period of time.' And he doesn't say anything.

"So he stores all of his things in her parents' basement in New Jersey for the summer, and every time her father goes down there, he says, 'What's that funny smell? It wasn't here last year.' And when my friend gets married in the fall, and they load the car with the guy's boxes from the basement, the terrible smell follows them for three hundred straight miles up the New York Thruway.

"So they get to their honeymoon apartment and she starts to unpack the boxes and, to her astonishment, there are six weeks' worth of dirty dishes — still unwashed! The mold is so thick she's afraid it'll crawl out and devour the wedding presents. And since then, the guy hasn't changed a bit! Is there any hope for a man who would do a thing like that to his bride?"

"Just one question," said Greg. "These 'friends' of yours wouldn't happen to be you and Ralph, would they?"

"How did you know?" I said, astonished.

"A psychologist's intuition," said Greg, "and sharing a locker with Ralph at the gym."

"The amazing part of it," I said, "is that Ralph is impeccably neat and organized at work. But he can slovenize his own home in five minutes."

"You have to realize, though," said Greg, "that the problem is really yours. Ralph is not in distress; *you* are. The alternatives I see are: first, we help you to accept Ralph as he is; or second, try to subtly change Ralph's behavior at home toward greater tidiness."

"Let's change Ralph," I said.

"Or," continued Greg, "there's a third alternative, which might be easiest yet."

"Yes?" I said.

"You could become a slob too."

That, however, I felt would set a bad precedent in our marriage (letting wrong triumph over right), though there were many moments when I wondered whether the solution might be simply to out-sloth Ralph on a long-term basis. He might *say* he doesn't care if the kitchen counters are ever cleaned or not, but having to cook with one hand and fight off the roaches with the other might change his mind.

Or then again, maybe it wouldn't. Before he got married, Ralph's brother Steve had an apartment in Greenwich Village that had so many roaches that, in all fairness, they should have paid half the rent. (The place was right over an Italian restaurant, so it wasn't *all* his fault.) And every morning when Steve left for work he'd say, "Good-bye, roaches," trying to build up a rapport with them. (He always maintained that they gave him the feeling he wasn't alone and were much less trouble than a dog.)

Now, I'll have to admit that Ralph has improved some since our first year. But old habits seem to die hard. It wasn't more than six months ago that a disgruntled Ralph was sent into the kitchen to clean orange juice off the wall after having used the blender without the top. Over the sound of running water came the words, "My mother never minded cleaning up after me." The water stopped.

"She loved me."

Styles of getting angry (or, Mount St. Helens meets the Rock of Gibraltar)

My sister, Marie, used to say, "When Louise gets angry, we all run down to the basement and hide behind the furnace."

That, of course, was not true. What she meant was behind the heating-oil tank. There wasn't room behind the furnace.

I've never had any trouble feeling anger. Expressing it constructively was the hard part.

Ralph always likened me to a volcano when I got angry. I tended to let things build up. Then one day Ralph would commit a relatively minor offense, like leaving the butter out, and get annihilated.

Ralph, like my sister, Marie, tended to be more of a slow-burn type. When he got angry, he'd never explode. He'd just glower at you for days until you couldn't stand it anymore. Fortunately, over the past ten years, he's gotten much more expressive, and I've learned to cool it. Most of the time, anyway.

Actually, when I'm really angry, I'm not loud or violent. Just all-inclusive. For example, I remember the time during the first year we were married when I'd been having a terrible problem with our car. We'd spent a lot of money on a deluxe tune-up, which the mechanic had assured us would solve our problems. Since then, the car had stopped dead six times.

I tried to be very calm but emphatic about it the first five times, just like my assertiveness-training book said: Explain your position and be clear about what you want done. The sixth time, however, as the car was towed into the station, I totally lost my cool and went storming into the station owner's office and practically buried him in molten lava.

This was a mistake. It was a mistake because even though I was the "wronged" party, I ended up spending the rest of the week apologizing to him for what I said about his integrity, the intelligence of his mechanics, his mother, his mechanics' mothers, his IQ at birth, the decor of the station, and where (and with what) he could put his tune-ups.

It also does not help community relations.

Always full of remorse and new resolve after I do something like this, I keep telling myself: Stick with the issue! Deal with tensions at the time! Don't let them build up! Don't throw in stuff that happened more than four years ago! And leave the person's relatives out of it!

Some things in life are just so hard.

A call for help

Maybe it would help you to understand Ralph better if I told you that he just seems to have a way with information operators.

Why this is so I have never been able to figure out. Maybe it's because Ralph genuinely loves information operators. There is no doubt in his mind that they are his friends and that if he has a problem, they will want to help him with it. Like his mother. ("Ma Bell" is the right word when it comes to Ralph and the phone company.)

Ralph calls the operator about things that have nothing to do with phone numbers. Like, I remember once when we were on vacation, I said, "Where should we eat tonight?"

"I don't know," said Ralph. "Let's call the operator and ask her what's good." Ralph maintains that he gets much better advice on good restaurants from information operators than from travel guides.

Maybe I'm just jealous. I can't get a street address out of an information operator no matter what I say. If I called the operator and asked her about a good place to eat, she'd say, "Have you lost your buttons, sweetpea?" and hang up.

Early in our marriage, an incident occurred that was a good example of Ralph's amazing relationship with operators. We were out of town and had heard of a little Italian place in the area. We couldn't remember the name exactly, but we'd been told that the cook used to work at Mama Leone's in New York. No one at the little motel we were staying at could help us.

"I'll call the information operator," said Ralph.

"Ralph," I said, "you can't do that! Without the name, what are you going to ask her?"

But Ralph, all childlike faith, was already on the phone.

"Yes, operator," he said, "I'm trying to locate an Italian restaurant in Bellevue. I thought the name was Joe's or Gino's, but I can't find either of those in the county directory."

"I don't see it either," said the operator. "Are you sure of the names?"

"Well, I thought it was Joe's or Gino's," said Ralph. "It's supposed to be really good."

"Ralph," I hissed, "would you stop harassing that poor woman? There is no way you're going to find it!"

"Wait a minute," said the operator. "I think I might know the place you mean."

"Oh, have you eaten there?" said Ralph.

"The name wasn't Joe's but something very similar," she said. "And the food was terrific."

"Maybe that's it," said Ralph. "I heard the cook used to work at Mama Leone's in New York."

"Ralph," I hissed, "would you give up? God forbid somebody should want some information!"

"Mama Leone's!" said the operator. "Wow."

"As long as you've eaten there," said Ralph, "do you remember what's good?"

"Well, it's been quite a while," said the operator. "My boyfriend took me there. I think, though, I had the chicken marsala."

"Do you think I'd need a reservation?" said Ralph.

"In Bellevue?" said the operator.

"Would you be able to give me directions from the motel?" said Ralph.

"For heaven's sake, Ralph," I said. "This is the info operator, not the automobile club!"

"I'm not sure of the exact street," said the operator. "I don't live in the Bellevue area myself. But let me see if anyone else here knows." She was back in a minute. "Here's why we couldn't find the listing," she said. "One of the girls says it's called *Uncle* Joe's."

The operator gave Ralph directions, then she and Ralph chatted amiably for several minutes before finally saying their good-byes, Ralph wishing her all the best, and she wishing Ralph a good meal.

"Ralph," I said afterward, "I will never understand why they don't just hang up on you."

Ralph looked puzzled. "Why would they want to do that?" he said.

A little savoir saves you a lot of fare

Even about nonacademic things, I have always seemed to learn the hard way.

I remember, for example, getting a job as a peon in a New York City hospital the summer before we got married. Actually, the job was fun, but this hospital was not exactly a model of efficiency, as I discovered when it took me eight weeks to get my first paycheck. Turned out the check had to be OK'd by about 160 people, who tended to be sick or on vacation or recently declared mentally incompetent. It was certainly no surprise to me when several years later New York almost defaulted.

After I'd been there about seven weeks and was really out of money, my clinic and the neighboring one decided to have a joint luncheon in honor of three departing employees. I didn't know anyone very well, being a college student just filling in as summer help, but it sounded like fun, so that morning, I withdrew $2.00 from my ravaged savings. (Usually I only took out $1.00, but I wanted to live it up.)

I suppose I should have known that they didn't mean the turkey plate at Bickford's, but the first thing I noticed when we all got to the restaurant was that the only thing I could afford was the small clam chowder, $1.50. (With tax and tip it would come to $1.83. That would still leave me $.17 for a light supper.)

What I didn't know was that when this group went out, they didn't lunch, they debauched. (*Ben Casey* was never like this.) For three hours, they ate and drank their way through cocktails, clams casino, oyster stew, lobster Newburg, appropriate wine, chocolate mousse, and crème de menthe—accompanied by numerous toasts to the departing, and gradually deteriorating into camp songs.

Louise, meanwhile, had a small clam chowder and twenty-six packages of oyster crackers.

It was the longest afternoon of my whole life. There I am salivating into my handbag watching people eat lobster, and this doctor next to me keeps saying, "I never met anybody who liked oyster crackers so much."

I can't express how happy I was when, several millennia later, the bill came. And just as I was asking the doctor next to me for change of a dollar (so I could give them exact change and not lose my $.17; very savvy, I thought), this guy at the head of the table says, "Of course, we all want to treat the honorees, so I think it will come out right if everyone else contributes sixteen dollars."

I guess I must have developed a sudden facial tic or started making weird animal noises, because eventually, my boss looked down from her end of the table and said, "Wait a minute. I think Louise here is in an awkward social situation."

I was saved! She'd figured it out! I resumed breathing.

"I forgot that Louise hasn't been paid yet," she continued. "Would anyone be willing to lend her the money?"

It cost me $16.00 — a veritable fortune to me at the time — but at least I learned a powerful and important lesson about going out to eat with a large group of people:

Always order the most expensive thing on the menu.

Of mice and men

You never really know a person until you see him under extreme stress.

Take my husband, Ralph, for example.

After two years of courtship, I thought he was the Rock of Gibraltar. I used to stand by in open-mouthed amazement as he unflinchingly performed feats of daring, like stopping midway up a steep hill in a stick-shift car, or lighting the pilot light on the water heater with a short match, or driving in the garment district in Manhattan.

That was, of course, until the arrival of Ben.

We were sitting there at the dinner table one night when Ralph looked into the kitchen and suddenly froze rigor mortisly. Realizing he'd had a stroke, I got up to call an ambulance.

"There's a rat on the stove," hissed Ralph, still paralyzed.

In my mind, I immediately pictured this massive creature with a sneer on its face and a long, filthy tail hanging in my leftover tomato sauce.

Ralph had meanwhile developed signs of brain-stem dysfunction and was making guttural sounds. From his reaction, I knew this must be one enormous rat.

I peered cautiously around the corner into the kitchen. Perched on the stove looking over my eggplant was the cutest little brown mouse I'd ever seen.

I'll admit to a prior fondness for mice. In the seventh grade, I brought home a black mouse from the school science lab with the written guarantee of my science teacher that it could not possibly live for more than two months and please make its last days pleasant ones.

"Snowball" (the mouse) resided in the living room in a cage that I cleaned once every six months whether it needed it or not, dousing the cage between cleanings with Apple Blossom perfume, which I purchased with my allowance for something like twenty-nine cents a gallon.

He thrived on my father's French cooking, developing a particular fondness for *poulet en cocotte bonne femme* saved from my plate and served in Chock full o' Nuts measuring cups.

Three years later, however, my father, cumulatively driven wild by the combined smells of Apple Blossom and Snowball droppings and by the incessant sounds of a squeaky exercise wheel, opted to have Snowball dropped from the family circle.

So I was pleased to see Ben. He provided companionship when Ralph worked late and gave Ralph an incentive to clean up after himself in the kitchen, to which Ralph was otherwise morally opposed.

But Snowball had at least had the decency to stay in his cage and not leave droppings in my silverware tray or gnaw on my dish towels. Ben had not been versed in territoriality.

I came home one night to find Ralph practically hyperventilating in the hallway after Ben had wandered casually out of the living room heat register and walked over Ralph's foot en route to the kitchen.

"This mouse," said Ralph, "has chutzpah." It also turned out to have a fondness for matzoh meal. (That's when we began calling him Ben Gurion.)

Reluctantly I agreed with Ralph that Ben had to go.

A veritable banquet of Ben's favorite foods was arranged in mousetraps. I wanted his last meal to be a good one.

Still, on the day that Ben succumbed, there was no consoling me, even as I took the silverware and the dish towels from temporary storage in the refrigerator and put them back in their usual drawers.

Ralph, however, was transformed.

"I never knew you were so afraid of rodents," I said to him. "I hope this will make you more sympathetic in the future to *my* fears."

"But," said Ralph, "yours are irrational."

Musical myths

In my family, I was the musical one. That meant I wasn't quite as tone deaf as the rest of them.

None of us could carry a tune to save our lives. I, however, was the only one who knew it. (It was once suggested that our family sing-alongs be recorded and used to disperse riots.)

As the family's great musical hope, I took eight years of piano lessons and four years of organ. Ralph was very impressed when my mother informed him of that when he came to pick me up one night for a date during our courtship. The reason I mention all this is that Ralph was at the time supporting himself through school as a semiprofessional musician. Finding someone who shared his interest in music was *very* important to him.

"Louise!" he said, surprised and delighted. "You've never told me you were an accomplished musician."

"Louise was even secretary of the Organ Club," added Mother proudly, never one to leave bad enough alone.

"The *what?*" said Ralph.

You see, my high school was one of the few in the area that offered free organ lessons. In return, students were expected on a rotating basis to play a little schmaltz during the entrance to and egress from school assemblies, and to participate in the Organ Club.

Of course, the main problem with the Organ Club was its name. How anyone would have stuck a bunch of innocent (well, sensitive, anyway) high-school kids with a double entendre like that, I'll never know.

What I *do* know is that for three straight years, every time an

Organ Club meeting was announced in homeroom, the alphabetical creepo sitting next to me would lean over and leer, "Hey, Louise, wanna play *my* organ?"

The Organ Club did, however, have one highly compensating quality: field trips. At least once a month, we got the whole day off to go visit a distinguished organ.

Some of my fondest memories of high school were those field trips. Eight of us (and of course, Dr. Watkins, the organ teacher) would take off in the school station wagon, singing and laughing and engaging in such cute antics as posting signs on the side windows at tollbooths like, "Help! We are being kidnapped by the bald man in the front seat!"

And in the delectable forbidden glory of midweek afternoons, we saw the rolling hills of Connecticut, the hustle and bustle of New York City, the lovely wooded countryside of northern New Jersey and Pennsylvania, stopping to lunch at inexpensive (but to us, exotic) places. Some of them, like Tad's Steak House in New York, I remember as if it were yesterday: $1.49 for steak, sizzling on the grill right in front of you, and baked potato with lots of melted butter, and salad with four choices of dressing!

And the smorgasbord in Allentown! Luscious salads of every description, meatballs in succulent sauces, butterfly shrimps, and all the chocolate eclairs you could eat!

Oh. And we also saw some very nice organs.

As I started out saying, there was my mother standing there making me out to be some kind of virtuosa, and what could I say? The truth of the matter was, of course, that I wasn't. A lot of people don't realize that you can be absolutely terrible even after eight years of piano and four years of organ, but I am a living testament to it.

I'm not devoid of musical ability. I have just enough ear to know that I don't have one.

When the truth finally came out, after, alas, we were married, Ralph at first couldn't believe what had motivated me to persist in music lessons for eight such relentlessly unpromising years. The answer to that was simple: regardless of talent, I *loved* music. Besides which, I couldn't bear to disappoint my family — they were so proud of having someone in the family who was "musical." They were sure I could have been a concert pianist if I'd wanted to be.

And OK, I'll admit it. I loved being the family music authority. I thrived on all that respect. Then, for reasons still unknown to me, I went and ruined it all by marrying a musician.

Several years ago, before she died, my mother was out visiting us. "Louise," she said, "why don't you play something on the piano?" Mother freely admitted that music just sounded like noise to her, but she enjoyed watching the keys move.

How do you tell your mother, who thinks you could have been a concert pianist, that after eight years of piano and four years of organ, your husband won't let you lay hands on a musical instrument while he is in the house?

In one of my more indignant moments, I said to Ralph, "I'll have you know that I once won a prize from my music teacher."

"For what?" said Ralph cheerfully. "Paying your bill?"

Actually, it was for writing the best report about a composer. I won a makeup kit for brunettes. I'm a blond.

To this day, Ralph has never quite forgiven me for not being the musician I made myself out to be. And OK, so I may not have the musical talent of Van Cliburn. Or maybe even Van Cliburn's cat. But to be perfectly honest, I think I *am* more musical than Ralph gives me credit for.

One day, for example, we were sitting at breakfast and a loud buzzer sounded from the laundry room.

"Sounds like the dryer is done," said Ralph.

"No, that's the washing machine off balance," I said, without even glancing up from the morning paper.

I can tell a tone when I have to.

Issues of Early Marriage

When a couple first gets married, there follows a certain period of adjustment—a time for the partners to get to know the real, rather than the idealized, versions of each other and to begin to deal with some of the early tasks of marriage. These tasks might include separating from the family of origin, developing effective communication, mastering domestic skills, working out the distribution of power, reconciling religious or cultural differences, establishing a functioning household, and resolving problems that arise from the partners' individual personalities.

Some couples do these things better than others.

A little communication is a wonderful thing

If there was one thing that both Ralph and I were hesitant to do in the early stages of our marriage, it was to ruin the other person's good time.

In recent years, however, we have discovered more things that we did during that era that we both hated every minute of but didn't say anything about because we thought the other person was really enjoying it.

Take our first camping trip, for example.

Now, not long after we got married, Ralph and I moved to Colorado and it seemed like everybody we knew there went camping. So we decided if everybody else liked it so much, it must be fun. Why I didn't learn the fallacy of that argument with skiing, I don't know.

We didn't have any camping equipment or any money to buy camping equipment, so we just took the foam-rubber mattress off our bed and threw it into the old Ford-wagon-my-father-gave-us-as-a-wedding-gift-so-I-wouldn't-have-to-drive-Ralph's-Corvair-which-he-regarded-as-unsafe, packed up a coolerful of food, and took off for what we had every expectation would be a blissful communion with nature.

It took me until the second morning to realize I was not having fun.

At first, I liked to blame my lack of enthusiasm on the fact that the campgrounds were absolutely jammed. I mean, you had to wait forty-five minutes to pay your twenty-five cents to use the shower. (The alternative was the nice, picturesque lake, which the guidebook failed to mention was forty-eight degrees.) But I knew deep in my heart that we could have had the whole national forest to ourselves and I wouldn't have liked it any better.

For some years, however, I was able to sustain the illusion that it was simply because we did not have the right equipment or expertise. That lasted until two years later when we went backpacking with some friends who had down sleeping bags, caught their fish in the stream — the whole schtik. By the third day, however, I would have traded the sleeping bags, the fish, *and* the friends for a chance to stand in line for the warm shower.

I am a person who loves the great outdoors by day. And the great *in*doors by night.

But there I was out in the boonies during that first trip with the prospect of six more days of food that was either charred or raw and six more nights of little urchins peering in the windows of the station wagon at 5:00 A.M. and saying, "Look, Mommy. What a funny camper!"

But Ralph seemed to be having such a good time that I didn't want even to suggest to him that I wasn't. This was not all altruism, by the way. We'd only been married a year at the time and I didn't want him to think I wasn't rugged and adaptable. It's incredible the heroic lengths newlyweds will go to misrepresent themselves.

As I remember it, it was the fifth night of this trip when we rolled into the next campground on our itinerary. "Unbroken vista," the guidebook said. What the guidebook *didn't* say was that it was ten thousand feet up and below freezing at night in August. There was *snow* on the ground.

Well, we duly set about finding our campsite and Ralph unloads the car and I start a fire to cook the evening's charcoal extravaganza, and the sky is cloudy and the sun has gone down behind the mountain and the temperature is dropping fast, and we put on all the clothes we own but we're still shivering, and I'm being very amiable even though I'd sell my college education not to be (a) spending the night on this polar icecap or (b) eating this junk, and finally it's time to sit down at the picnic table for supper.

"Ketchup?" I say pleasantly.

"Yes, thank you," says Ralph equally pleasantly, drowning his burger in it. And we're sitting there eating away silently until I notice Ralph's eyes light up suddenly.

"Penny for your thoughts," I say.

"Oh, it was nothing," insists Ralph. But the brightness is still there.

"I'll make it a quarter," I say.

Ralph's eyes light up brighter than ever. "If we leave right now," he blurts out excitedly, "we can be home by midnight!"

And we both jump up and start throwing our stuff back into the car, without even packing it up or anything, and Ralph is jubilantly throwing his burger to the neighbor's dachshund and I'm dancing around pouring Kool-Aid on the fire.

Two minutes later, we were gone.

Learning to cook (or, Never say die)

Every bride makes mistakes.

That's how you learn. I haven't met a woman yet who didn't have a tragic bride story—some stories almost universal, others more unusual.

Is there a bride amongst us who has not confused a bulb for a clove of garlic and ended up with a beef stew that could wipe out New Jersey? Who has not mixed white and colored items in the washer and sent her husband off to work in pink undies? Who has not beaten down a bread dough after the final rise, then baked it? (With a coat of shellac, this last one makes a great paperweight, by the way.)

We'd only been married two and one half months at the time of our first Thanksgiving, a time frame that Ralph still remembers as one long attack of indigestion. In one sense I was your stereotypical bride: a terrible cook. Ralph, however, was already quite proficient in the kitchen, having had his own apartment for several years, and as the hours wore by, he became increasingly anxious to take over. But I kept reminding him that I'd never learn to cook if he didn't give me a chance. I wasn't all that interested, frankly, but I thought I *should* know how.

Meanwhile, I experimented with such traditional delicacies as corn on the cob (boiled for an hour to make sure it was done), roast pork au raw, and recipes of my own creation such as Beans Quinine, which I've always meant to try again except with club soda. I once made a chicken casserole that had so much flour it jammed the garbage disposal.

The menu I planned for our first Thanksgiving dinner included a turkey with all the trimmings, vegetables, clam chowder, and my first homemade apple pie.

Unfortunately, it was also right about time for my midsemester exams and term papers at college, but I was confident I could cook and formulate term-paper topics simultaneously. (I think this was where I went wrong with cooking. It hadn't occurred to me that it required you to pay attention.)

The day before Thanksgiving, I started with the apple pie. With a history paper to write that day too, peeling the apples seemed like a frivolous waste of time. Who was going to see them, anyway? And at the last minute, I discovered I was also missing some strange spice called cornstarch, but having eliminated many optional spices (like nutmeg) before, I strongly suspected I could do without it.

I did notice, however, that when the pie was assembled, the apples seemed to be swimming around in a rather thin, runny yuk, not at all like the thick, gooey pies at the bakery. I could see this clearly, as I hadn't made enough dough for a complete top crust and had thus improvised a rather simple latticework top — two strips lengthwise, one crosswise — which unfortunately kept sinking from view into the apple goop.

I assumed at this point that maybe the pie would thicken as it cooked. But it didn't. So I poured off the excess runny yuk and pinned my hopes on the remainder thickening as it cooled. (Hope springs eternal.) It was then that I realized that the apples, now shriveling up without the liquid, were inexplicably still raw. The only thing I could figure out was that maybe the large broiler pan on the lower shelf was blocking heat.

Deciding that the pie needed to cook more and that I shouldn't have poured off the runny yuk, I poured apple cider over the dried-up apples as a last resort and shoved the whole thing back in the oven. This, at least, had the promising effect of making the latticework dough pieces float to the top again. So much for the pie.

On Thanksgiving Day, I made the turkey and the rest of the meal, and our friend Mark came over to join us. Ralph took pictures of me taking the turkey, which was listing forty degrees to starboard with its feet waving in the air, out of the oven. I was poised to take a picture of Ralph carving, when the smile disappeared from his face. Suddenly he peered into the turkey cavity and pulled out a steaming, soggy bag full of gizzards and innards.

I couldn't for the life of me figure out why the butcher would have put them there without telling me. It also explained why only a quarter of the stuffing would go in, even using brute force.

"How's the clam chowder?" I asked, as Ralph and Mark sampled it.

"Well," said Mark choosing his words carefully, "it's delicious. Of course, you really have to like Worcestershire sauce to appreciate it."

The salad, everyone agreed, was delicious. I have always made wonderful salads.

The pie? What can I say?

It received a proper Christian burial.

Resolving religious differences

Funny I should mention Christian burials.

There is a popular rumor that the two topics people are most reluctant to discuss are sex and money. Both wrong. It's religion.

Ralph's and my courtship and early marriage were plagued with problems about religion. Or ostensibly about it, anyway.

I remember one night during our engagement Ralph and I went to see the movie version of *Romeo and Juliet* and afterward walked silently hand-in-hand through Central Park, tears streaming down our faces, identifying thoroughly with the trials and tribulations that lovers endure. We were heavily into parental-interference problems ourselves.

From my point of view, I couldn't see what the Montagues and Capulets were getting so excited about. After all, Romeo was a good-looking boy — athletic, no acne or major physical defects — had identical religious beliefs and similar socioeconomic background, and even had a comparable home in the same neighborhood. (They could go to *both* families for Christmas.) I mean, Ralph's and my parents would have been ecstatic if we had been a bit more interested in homogamy of values.

As I remember it, about the only thing Ralph and I had in common during our engagement was that we wanted to marry each other. Although certainly not the most significant of our differences, the arena in which Ralph and I and assorted parents acted out our conflicts was religion. Ralph was of Russian-Jewish heritage; and I was the product of a conservative French-Catholic father and a liberal ex–DAR Protestant mother. We were definitely a mixed bag.

Religious differences are a convenient issue because they're so definable: you either "are" or you "aren't," and it made no difference that none of the four parental members of this international melange had set foot in a house of worship in some years. Suddenly both of our homes became hotbeds of orthodoxy.

Ralph's mother was quick to point out that her objections to me should not be taken personally. It was just that in her opinion, there was no lower form of animal life than a shiksa who wanted to marry her son.

My father was more pragmatic about it. "So what are you going to say to your son's teacher? 'Please excuse little Jimmy for Chanukah, Christmas, and the Feast of the Immaculate Conception'?"

My mother's main objections actually had nothing to do with religion. She liked Ralph very much but thought I was much too young to get married. If I was really serious about this relationship, she suggested, why didn't Ralph and I just live together? (In my house, you rebelled by subscribing to the *Ladies' Home Journal.*)

When my mother married my father, I should mention, she agreed to adhere to the basic tenets of Catholicism. After three children in three and a half years, however — all of us living on ninety dollars a month from the GI Bill—she underwent a profound spiritual change and became one of the world's foremost proponents of birth control. Mother also began to feel that we should have exposure to other ways of thinking about religion, and, while we duly went to Mass and studied our catechism, Mother also took us to every other church available. As teenagers, Pierre and I chose to be confirmed as Catholics, but Marie decided to be Episcopalian. Ultimately, however, we married a Church of England, a Southern Baptist, and a Jew. Marie once described our family as a walking universal Western religion.

Having made an interreligious marriage themselves, my parents repeatedly stressed the need for Ralph and me to resolve certain fundamental issues *before* we got married, or at least agree to disagree. I'll have to admit that their insistence on this matter is probably one reason we're still married. We were into happy idealism at the time and felt that no conflict would be too hard to resolve, because we loved each other.

That was until we began making plans for the wedding, an affair which was canceled somewhere in the vicinity of forty times. Finding someone of a religious persuasion to marry us was somewhat akin to finding an illegal abortionist. (One of our proposed candidates once whispered to us that he knew of a rabbi in Jersey City who "did that sort of thing.") The major problem was that the very few who would consider performing the ceremony persisted in requiring conversions, extracting promises, or engaging us in discussion about the Comings and Goings of certain religiously significant individuals, and it really hit the fan.

By the time we got married (by a justice of the peace), there was no doubt in our minds what we were going to do Fridays, Sundays, and postpartums. Despite some occasional rocky moments, it has been relatively easy going since.

Our first holiday season together, however, did pose a few knotty problems. In the weeks before we got married, my relationship with Ralph's parents had become a bit, shall we say, strained. (They announced they were boycotting the ceremony, and I said that was OK because if they showed up, I'd call the police.) Suffice it to say that by the time the holiday season rolled around three months later, Ralph and I were still very reluctant to step on each other's religious toes. So we launched the season with Thanksgiving, shifted into Chanukah, then slid directly into Christmas.

Now, this could have been a very expensive proposition, giftwise, but fortunately we hit upon the first of several simple principles: It's the thought that counts. This was a very convenient principle, because at the time, we were very long on thoughts and very short on money.

Second, both of us had noticed that the real excitement of the holiday season was fantasizing about all those mysterious, colorful packages under the tree. It almost didn't matter what was in them so long as you were surprised.

Ergo, third, it was only logical that if it is the thought that counts, then just because a gift has been given once doesn't mean it can't be given again, even to the same person. Just so long as they're surprised (and they usually are when they get something they already own).

It all made so much *sense*.

So under our Christmas-Chanukah tree-bush, there evolved three classes of gifts. First, of course, were the bona fide gifts, the ones you went to a store and paid real money for and that were aboveboard and traditional and legitimate. There were maybe three or four *very* modest ones of those.

Then there were the bogus gifts, which constituted anything you came by legally at no cost, like the green plastic horn that came free with the large size of Crest or the prize in the cereal box or the free sample of anal suppositories you got in the mail. *Nothing* escaped our eagle eyes.

The third — and largest — category was the recycled wedding gifts. Now, we got a lot of nice things for our wedding, and frankly, they were almost as much fun the second time around as the first. Some of them even got given three or four times. For example, I remember during Chanukah I gave Ralph the sterling-silver candlesnuffer one night and he secretly wrapped it up again and gave it back to me the next night; then I disguised it in a liquor-store carton and gave it back to him for Christmas.

And, of course, we were each surprised each time we got it, because neither of us expected to get the snuffer, originally a gift from my Aunt Martha, once, much less four times. (I think that was also the only action that snuffer ever saw. Mercifully, it was stolen.)

Naturally, you never knew ahead of time what kind of gift your spouse had in store for you that night, so it got pretty exciting. We ended up having a good time and spent a minimum of money — mostly for wrapping paper, I think.

We were both a little relieved when it was all over, though. By the next year, I could cook a Passover dinner, Ralph could string Christmas lights, and it didn't seem like much of a problem anymore.

Domestic skills

Actually, I probably shouldn't be too critical of Ralph's laundry skills after what I did to the llama.

In my defense, I was a very young bride. Still in college. Inexperienced in the ways of the world. Living among strangers with no one to guide me.

Of course, it wasn't a whole llama. It was just the skin of one, which my parents had gotten as a gift and which I persuaded them to lend me for my first apartment.

Naturally, a white, long-haired llama skin gets very dirty after a while. So the next time I called home, I asked my mother if it might be washable. She said she thought it was.

Now, afterward, Mother insisted that what she meant by "washable" was that I might put the llama skin ever so carefully into a bathtub full of cold water with the tiniest drop of Woolite and poke it very gently from time to time with my index finger.

Mother says she *never* meant that I should take it down to the basement laundry room and throw it in the washer with a week's worth of dirty underwear.

Imagine my utter dismay when I went down to transfer it to the dryer and found that the backing on the skin that held it all together had somehow disintegrated and I had a whole washerload of wet, hairy llama with all our dainties hopelessly — and I mean hopelessly — entangled within.

I was miserable about it. The waste! Not only had I ruined this beautiful skin, but this meant that the donor llama had died in vain. (I had a soft heart and was into ecology at the time.)

Not to mention that it wasn't even my llama. "What am I going to tell the folks?" I wailed, as I stood there tearfully hacking it out of the washer with a bowie knife.

Unlike the Thanksgiving dinner, this was one of those mistakes that hangs around to haunt you. It was *weeks* before we could extricate all the laundry from the tangled mass of hair, which we kept conveniently piled on top of our dresser. In the morning Ralph would sometimes stick his head out of the bathroom where he was shaving and yell, "I'm out of shorts. Would you cut me a pair out of the llama?"

Now I only buy synthetics. They make you feel less guilty.

Finding compatible leisure-time activities
(or, How I would have sold my soul
to get off the ski slopes)

During the first year we were married, several of my ex-friends talked Ralph and me into trying skiing.

"You'll love it," they said. "Just look at all the people who ski. They can't all be crazy."

I agreed. There were probably at least a dozen sane ones

who were there only under duress and were hating every minute of it.

Ralph, being highly coordinated and athletic, was very eager to try it. "It'll be a terrific social thing besides the exercise," he pointed out. "We'd have a basis with people, a common interest. Deep friendships are not made on weekly Saturday-night-chicken-cacciatore dinners alone, you know."

I agreed. We needed to find a new menu.

"So we'll go?" said Ralph.

I chose my words carefully.

"No."

Don't get me wrong. I love exercise. Always have. I walk seven or eight miles at a stretch. Swim as often as I can. Used to fence and play squash. But I am definitely a warm-weather type with a fear of heights that would make some of Freud's more tragic cases look normal.

You can imagine how elated I was when Ralph presented me with a complete ski outfit for my birthday, including skis, poles, and bindings. I should mention that we were both students at the time, on an extremely tight budget.

"Thank you, Ralph," I said, deciding what I'd exchange it all for at my earliest convenience. "But I'd be less than honest if I didn't say that your gift stinks and I hate you."

"Gosh," said Ralph, acting all hurt and innocent. "I guess maybe it was a mistake to buy it all on sale."

Well, with an investment like that, there was no other choice. We had to go skiing.

Ralph is a terrific guy, mind you, but the concept of someone not enjoying something he enjoys is totally beyond the scope of his imagination.

"Isn't it great!" he would exclaim from the top of the mountain, while I was breathing into the paper bag that the Ski Patrol had prescribed for my massive paralytic anxiety attacks. The bag worked wonders getting me to stop hyperventilating, but it's harder to ski with both poles in one hand.

No more pathetic sight hath man observed than a soggy, sobbing, terror-stricken me, dressed like a pregnant butterball, wobbly legs spread obscenely in perpetual snowplow, making my reluctant way straight down the mountain at a quarter-mile per hour with Ralph following along yelling, "You're doing great! Turn! Turn!"

No greater epithets has man ever heard than those I uttered at Ralph at five-second intervals. Except for the fact that I was the owner of this large, unsolicited pile of ski equipment, I would never have gone back. But Ralph was *sure* I'd begin to like it if I gave it a chance. (He loved it from the first minute.) He exacted a promise from me that I'd go fifteen times, and take lessons.

And true to my word, I did.

"Well?" said Ralph at the end of that time.

"Where do I sell my skis?" I said tersely. (The terseness was partly because my larynx was frozen to my esophagus.)

"But you're getting so much better!" said Ralph.

What Ralph never understood is that you can lead a horse to water, but you can't make him drink. Especially if the horse is secretly pissed as hell.

"What I can't understand, Ralph," I said, "is why anyone with half his marbles would willingly and with forethought spend a bundle of money to get up at six-thirty in the morning and drive for hours over dangerous mountain passes just to go up to the top of a mountain where it is twenty below zero and fling his body over the edge."

"Because it's fun," said Ralph. "Look, if you really hate it, we'll sell your skis and look for another activity we can do together. You know, just the other day I passed a store where, if you buy the equipment, they give you free lessons in scuba diving."

I put the point of my ski to Ralph's throat.

"Don't you *dare*."

Money (or, What's mine is yours, what's yours is mine, until one of us comes into some assets)

Over the past ten years, Ralph and I have had a number of "discussions" about money, the number and ferocity of these, as I recall, being in direct proportion to how much we didn't have of it. Of course, like most newlyweds, we initially went through a blissful period when neither money nor any of life's hurdles was any object—halcyon days of long walks in the woods, sunset rowboat rides on the lake, romantic candlelit dinners.

Then on the fourth day, everything changed.

The issue we had our first financial fight about was, ironically enough, how much we should share our various assets. Now, this had never been much of an issue while we were engaged because neither of us *had* any assets. Both of us, as a matter of fact, were walking liabilities. (My father used to remark wistfully, as he wrote out his monthly check to the bank, that in only ten more years, my education would be mine.)

So assets had never been much of a problem. That is, until my mother gave me five shares of stock as a wedding gift. Mother felt strongly that women should have some money in their own names.

The way Ralph carried on, you'd think my mother had given me half-ownership in the federal mint.

"For heaven's sake, Ralph," I said at the time, "we couldn't pay six months' rent with these stocks. Calm down."

"I realize that and I *am* calm," said Ralph, who was so calm that the veins were standing out on his forehead. "It's not the money I am concerned about." Funny how it's never the money anyone's concerned about. "It's symbolic."

"Symbolic of what?" I said. (That's the trouble with marriage. Everything's symbolic. You practically have to be a psychoanalyst to figure out your marriage. Not that it means psychoanalysts have great marriages either. They just have a profound understanding of why theirs failed.)

"It is symbolic," said Ralph, "of the fact that your mother does not think our marriage will succeed. She is giving you something to fall back on when you leave me."

"You'd rather keep me barefoot and pregnant?" I said. "What's wrong with a woman having a little financial security?"

"A better question," sniffed Ralph, "would be, what's wrong with your mother?"

"Mother," I said defensively, "simply feels that the status of women will never really change until they free themselves from economic dependence on men."

"Evil, wicked, nasty, malicious men," said Ralph. "Tough break you women have getting supported your whole lives."

"Women with children, no money, and no job skills are in a very powerless position," I pointed out.

"So what are you worried about?" said Ralph. "You have no children, good job skills, and five lousy shares of stock. Doesn't your mother believe in trust, commitment, love?"

"Of course she does. But in a pinch, you can't eat any of them."

"Well, Harriet Beecher Stowe, are you saying you want all our assets to be separate?"

"Of course not. Everything we acquire together — a house or car, for example — should be in both our names."

"That doesn't seem fair to me," said Ralph. "You keep your stocks, but everything I earn we put in both our names."

"Everything I earn too. So what do you want me to do?"

"Put the stocks in both our names."

"But that would ruin the whole idea of the gift."

"So you'd rather ruin the whole idea of our marriage?"

It was months before we were able to come to any resolution of this argument. (I learned during this time that the fundamental problem with marriage is that there are only two votes.) Eventually we agreed that all money or assets that came our way from any source — including mother's stocks — would automatically become joint property.

I've never heard Mother sigh so deeply as when I told her.

Problems of
Everyday Living

In the quest to understand the marital relationship, it should be emphasized that it is often the seemingly trivial process of everyday living—rather than the response to a major crisis—that elucidates the relative role functions of the partners as well as the more profound dynamics of the relationship.

That is to say, it is the little things in life that make you crazy.

Moving

Every year around July, Ralph and I reminisce about our move from Colorado to California.

Actually, I'm still trying to analyze why everything went so wrong on that trip. Maybe it was Ralph's ambivalence about his two-year Navy commitment that led him to rupture his Achilles tendon playing tennis five days before he had to report for duty in San Diego. Maybe our cat, Harry, wouldn't have gone psychotic if the freight train in Glenwood Springs hadn't passed so close to the car. And maybe I, as the only hope for this mobile sanitarium, shouldn't have eaten the burrito from the roadside stand. All I know is that by the second day, Ralph, the relatively healthiest amongst us, was elected to drive.

And thus we wound our abysmal way across the country,

taking scheduled breaks for Ralph to take aspirin for his postsurgical spinal-anesthesia headache, unscheduled breaks for me to be sick, and carrying on scintillating travelogue commentaries like:

"Feeling any better?"

(Grunt.) "You?"

(Grunt.)

The third day we were bombing along at seventy miles an hour just outside of Zion National Park when I signaled Ralph to pull over.

"I can't right now," said Ralph. "Try to get your head out the window."

Alas, the harsh reality of life is that when you stick your head out the window to be sick at seventy miles an hour, it all blows right back in, splat against the back window.

"Did you have to do that?" said Ralph, pulling over. "Now I can't see out the back." I opened the car door and fell out into the bushes. Because of his cast, Ralph couldn't get out of the car without my help.

"Louise, get up," said Ralph anxiously from the driver's seat. "People will think you are dead."

"That's all right, I am very close to it," I said. After three days of nausea, I'd have done anything not to get back into a moving vehicle.

"I'm a little worried Harry will get out," said Ralph.

I raised my head from the roadside and peered into the back seat. Harry's rigid tail was still sticking up from underneath his litter box.

"Why don't you just leave Harry and me here and remember us fondly?" I said.

The California border at last. Even though we'd heard that they'd search us carefully for fruit and foliage (to protect local agriculture), they just took one look at Ralph's crutches and Harry's rigid tail and the back window that Ralph still couldn't see out of and they waved us through, without asking if we had oranges or anything.

Now, we'd never been to California before we moved here, but reports from the newspapers back in Colorado (and before that, in New York) had formed vague images in our minds of a land of eternal sunshine, swaying palm trees, exotic Spanish addresses, nude encounter groups, mass murders, and drive-in churches. So we were (with a couple of exceptions there) pretty excited.

At a conference some months before we left, Ralph had met a guy from Los Angeles who, upon hearing we were moving to San Diego, invited us to spend our first night on California soil with him and his wife.

You can imagine our delight when, after this dismal trip, we pulled up to a spacious, six-bedroom home with pool, Jacuzzi, sauna, and even a bathtub that could have fitted eight.

"I think I like California," I said, looking over the premises.

Our hostess, Myrna, seemed like a nice person, although nobody I had ever known dressed that way.

"I think I'll take a bath," I said after dinner. That huge tub had looked very inviting.

"That sounds like a wonderful idea," said Myrna. "I think we'll join you."

I laughed. These Californians really had a risqué sense of humor.

"Let me go turn on the water," said Myrna, taking off her green-and-yellow-and-orange-striped knee socks and her French beret.

I shot Ralph my "You take the back door and I'll take the front and I think we can make Iowa by morning" look.

He shrugged his "When in Rome, do as the Californians do" look.

I whizzed off my "That's easy for *you* to say. You have a cast on your leg and can't take a bath anyway" look.

He countered with his "They'll think you're inhibited" look.

I, of course, shot back my "I *am* inhibited" look. Especially after I haven't shaved my legs in a week and God knows what my underwear looks like.

"Are they catatonic or what?" said Myrna to her husband.

"Myrna," I said finally, "um, if it's all the same to you, I'd actually probably prefer to take a bath by myself."

"Oh, *sure*," said Myrna. "I keep forgetting you're not Californians yet. I mean, I used to be really hung-up too. But before you know it, you'll be into nude parties and group sex and having the time of your lives. It's California."

Ralph and I nervously exchanged our "Los Angeles Airport? What do you have going in an easterly direction?" look.

Well, finally we get to San Diego and, just when we think that our traumas are over (not to mention Harry's), we discover that there is virtually no rental housing where cats are permitted. Even the temporary housing at the Navy base where we were staying doesn't allow pets. (We smuggled Harry in anyway but I couldn't sleep, convinced Harry would be found out and shot.)

A basic difference between Ralph and me is that I would compromise my life to any lengths necessary for a beloved family pet. Ralph would not.

Now, finding rental housing that wasn't overpriced or condemnable was a problem even without a cat. Frankly, I couldn't understand what landlords had against cats. Cats tend to be very well behaved and Harry was especially so after our move. (He never regained all his marbles, poor thing, and spent most of his time smiling serenely at the woodwork.)

After days of searching, we were enormously relieved to finally find a place we could almost afford. We didn't lie about Harry. We just failed to mention him.

We were so careful to keep Harry out of sight when the landlady came around that we still don't know how she found out about him. Maybe the neighbors told her. Maybe she knew a meow coming from a linen closet when she heard one. Who knows. But one day, she came over and announced that either the cat went or we did.

(She didn't mean that literally, of course. I would have been glad to let Harry keep the place.)

"I guess we'll just have to move," I said to Ralph when she left.

"Are you kidding?" said Ralph. "You saw the places that allowed cats. A cat wouldn't live there."

I burst into tears.

"We'll try to find a good home for him," said Ralph consolingly.

"But who's going to take a three-year-old psychotic cat?" I said, tearfully digging Harry out of the linens.

"If no one does," said Ralph, the voice of masculine practicality, "then I'm afraid Harry will just have to go to the big litter box in the sky. I am not moving."

The day before Harry had to be out came around and still no one had answered our ad for "Beautiful three-year-old male cat, unusually quiet." I was inconsolable. But then, just as it seemed that there was no hope for Harry, the doorbell rang.

"I want to look at the cat," said the young woman in the white waitress uniform. She explained to Ralph that only yesterday, her three-year-old cat, named Felix, had succumbed under tragic circumstances. (He was flattened by a truck, I think.) Ralph handed her Harry.

"Felix," she said right off.

"His name is Harry," I said. Ralph kicked me in the ankle.

"Well, it *is*," I said. But she didn't seem to be noticing me anyway. She had her arms around Harry and was caressing him intently.

"I'll take him," she said softly. Several minutes later she left with Harry, looking as spaced as ever, in her arms.

"I'm so relieved we found a good home for him," said Ralph, closing the door. He looked at me sympathetically. "Hey, don't cry."

It's a rough life being a soft touch.

Wisdom teeth

At ten o'clock one morning, I settled into the dentist's chair to have my wisdom teeth extracted.

At 11:00 A.M., Ralph came to take home my remains.

I should mention that I was first advised to have my wisdom teeth out two years before this, and being a conscientious patient, I immediately made an appointment. But being even more cowardly than conscientious, I canceled that appointment and the following three.

"Louise," Ralph had said several weeks before, "I think you ought to make another appointment with Dr. Torture." (Not his real name.)

"It's not that I'm scared," I assured Ralph. "It's just that I've canceled so many times that I'm afraid he might be just mad enough to take out my teeth through my armpit."

The morning of the proposed extractions, I woke up and said to Ralph, "Ralph, why would a perfectly healthy person with all her marbles willingly and with forethought make herself sick?"

"Get up," said Ralph. Having gone through four previous last-minute cancellations, he was becoming a cruel and unfeeling person.

"You know, Ralph," I said, getting dressed, "you always read about people who go in for a removal of a hangnail and die from an anesthetic reaction. Happens to football players with knee injuries all the time."

"Get in the car," said Ralph.

"Would you want it on your conscience, Ralph?" I said in the car. "When I die on the table, will you say to yourself, 'She knew, and yet I made her do it?' You'll become an alcoholic and ruin a promising career. For your sake, let's turn back."

When we got to the oral surgeon's office, Ralph personally turned me over to him. "I suggest you make the incision through her armpit," said Ralph, and walked out.

"I think we agreed on IV sedation," said Dr. Torture. I liked the idea of sedation but not the IV. Fortunately, he hit me with the nitrous oxide first.

"How are you feeling?" asked Dr. Torture.

"Wonderful!" I said with a smile. It was my last smile for three days.

"Cheap date, huh?" said Dr. Torture. The man had a sense of humor. Maybe he'd forgiven me enough to go only through my ear instead of my armpit.

"Thith ith fun," I said with my thirty-pound tongue. That nitrous stuff was really a trip.

Waking up, however, was not nearly as much fun. I went home with a mouthful of gauze, a small pharmacy of prescription drugs, and my four teeth in a tiny manila envelope. I wasn't quite sure what to do with the teeth. ("Dear Emily Post: What is the proper way to display excised bodily organs?")

I took pain medicine for pain and antinausea medicine for the nausea caused by the pain medicine and antibiotics to prevent infection and mycostatin for the yeast infection caused by the antibiotic. Medical science is a vicious cycle.

But the third morning, I woke up feeling better and found my four teeth and their tiny packet gone. In their place were four shiny quarters and a note from someone purporting to be the tooth fairy telling me not to spend it all in one place.

The food we eat (and wish we hadn't)

People are so critical of each other's eating and drinking habits these days that it takes all the fun out of being slowly poisoned.

The basic problem as I see it is that medical science has proven beyond doubt that there is simply no orally consumable item that's good for you anymore.

That's why I've always admired our friend Stan, who continues to enjoy his food despite his wife's constant nagging that it will be the death of him. Stan allows how that's probably so, and lifting his next bite to his lips, cheerfully adds that when the time comes, he'd like his ashes spread on a hot-fudge sundae.

My theory is that since we all know that whatever we put in our mouths is going to do us in, the only way to cope with it psychologically is to focus all our anxiety on one or two food categories to be paranoid about, then eat everything else without fear.

The problem is that it's not enough just to avoid certain foods yourself. You have to ruin everybody else's good time about it too.

Don't get me wrong. I'm all for people taking care of their bodies. It's just that you can't entertain people anymore without them acting as if you're trying to kill them.

Take the dinner party we had one spring. I made what Ralph calls my Scampi Sclerosis. (OK, so it was a little rich. It was a special occasion.)

There wasn't one course that I served that night that at least one person didn't refuse with moral indignation. That, of course, immediately made some other guest nervously ask the first why he objected so strongly to shellfish (milk products/ fats/alcoholic beverages/caffeine/carbohydrates/refined sugars/ unrefined sugars/white flour/anything with cholesterol/non-organically grown produce).

To which the first guest would reply, "It clogs the heart (rots the liver/destroys the brain/eats away the stomach/screws up the blood sugar/is infiltrated with insecticides/isn't whole grained/causes hyperactivity in rats/is an endangered species)."

"I would appreciate it," I said finally, "if there would be no more discussion of food until the last carcinogen has been cleared away."

Now, I'm sure that any friends of mine who read this would hasten to point out that I, too, have had my moments of dietary concern. (It's only called food fanaticism when other people do it.) A couple of years ago, for example, I began to worry that Ralph and I were eating too much meat. When I wasn't worrying about animal fats clogging our arteries, I was worrying about cancer of the colon. And when I wasn't worrying about either of those, I worried about hormones added to animal feed and vague meat-induced "toxicities" darkly alluded to in health-food books. On a particularly good day, I could work up a spectacular worry about the cost.

I think part of all this worry had to do with the fact that I was soon to turn twenty-nine and was having a severe attack of incipient decrepitude.

I'd also just read an article called "How to Murder Your Husband" about housewives who unintentionally (?) do in their husbands by plugging up their coronary plumbing with rich gravies, creamy desserts, and pork roasts. (You could almost imagine some sobbing housewife in the courtroom and the prosecutor asking her to identify Exhibit A, the murder weapon: a pastrami sandwich.)

Even though I was concerned about our diet, it actually took me quite some time to make any concrete changes. The reason for this is that there were two individuals of our acquaintance who presented compelling evidence that diet may not have the influence it is thought to on health, that maybe health is largely a matter of constitution. These individuals were Ralph's parents.

One year when they were visiting, I said to them, "Mom and Pop, you're in your early seventies" — Ralph was an after-thought — "and you're both in perfect health. Neither of you takes a single medication, which is remarkable in your age group. A touch overweight perhaps, but Pop still does all his own gardening and home maintenance, including painting the house inside and out, and Mom walks and rides her bicycle for hours every day. So tell me, what have you been eating all these years?"

Know what they said? Chicken-fat sandwiches. (On rye, however, never white.) Also corned beef, an occasional steak, little snacks of fried chicken skin, Kosher hot dogs, smoked fish, cream cheese, whole milk, lots of starches, cooked vegetables (Mom's parents felt that raw greens were for cows, not people), butter, plenty of eggs, and some desserts. Mom smoked. Pop drank. This gave me pause.

But all things considered, I eventually decided that it would certainly not hurt to have meatless dinners at least two nights per week (preferably more). That same night I broached the subject with Ralph.

Now, I did not expect Ralph to be wild with joy. Ralph, you should know, has always been your hard-core, dyed-in-the-wool meat and potato-kugel man. He'd sooner go without electricity.

So I was not altogether surprised when my suggestion was met with a look that could have frozen a stone.

"Tell you what," I offered. "I'll let you choose the menus."

"That's like letting Socrates choose between hemlock and strychnine," muttered Ralph. (A terrible analogy, of course.)

The next day, I came home with two highly recommended vegetarian cookbooks. Vegetarian cookbooks, I discovered, are more than just recipes without meat. It's a whole different style.

In the entertainment-ideas section of one of them, I read with interest where the author maintained that serving dessert two hours after a meal "is especially recommended if grass is smoked socially at your house." Instantly you get a sense this is not going to be a meatless *Ladies' Home Journal* cookbook.

"So what are my choices?" grumbled Ralph the next evening.

"Well," I said, "I was thinking of either the herbed soybean bulgur casserole or the baked cottage-cheese squares."

"Goyisha food," muttered Ralph under his breath.

"Then, how about the roasted celery and wheat au gratin. Or here's one you'll like — bean stroganoff."

The recipes looked great—I've always preferred vegetables and salads over meat—but even I had to admit that the names could have used a little of the old Madison Avenue touch. And for a, shall we say, reluctant vegetarian like Ralph, I quickly realized that I should not use terms like stroganoff, usually associated with you-know-what.

So far Ralph had not responded. "All right," I said, "if you don't like any of those, here's one that sounds pretty normal. 'Eggplant bake.' Hey, where are you going?"

"Out for a sausage pizza," said Ralph.

After this inauspicious beginning, I did begin making several meatless dinners each week, which incidentally *I* thought were a huge improvement over our diet before. And even Ralph, after he'd tasted them, admitted that some of the dishes, like the mushroom curry, were really pretty good.

I don't want to imply, however, that I didn't have to pay a price for all this. There was nothing Ralph enjoyed more than to open the refrigerator door and announce, "Well, I think I'll have a little alkaline snack." Or to survey the array of vitamin pills in the medicine chest and remark, "Your problem, Louise, is that you're not getting enough vitamin E."

The ultimate problem, alas, was that for Ralph, if there was no meat, it just didn't feel like dinner. His stomach may have been full, but he was psychologically still hungry.

But I really thought I was converting Ralph over to lighter meals. That was until the night when, after a delicious repast of spinach quiche and fruit-and-nut salad, I caught Ralph out in the kitchen whipping up what he called "a bedtime snack": a double-decker knockwurst sandwich.

Ladies and gentlemen of the jury, I did my best.

The perverse nature of the automotive vehicle

I was always fascinated watching those crime shows where the bad guys run out of the bank with the loot, jump into a parked automobile waiting at the curb, turn on the ignition, and roar off down the street at sixty miles an hour.

I have never been very good at identifying makes of cars, particularly on a TV screen, but there was one thing I was always sure of about that vehicle.

It was not a Vega.

I would like to interject here that I used to like cars, I really did. They were nice to look at, offered an alluring line of gadgets, and looked infinitely more comfortable than a covered wagon. That, of course, was before I was forced to depend on one. In retrospect, I would have been better off with the covered wagon.

Frankly, cars and I got off to a terrible start.

The first year Ralph and I were married, we lived in a charming New England–style town in upstate New York. At least I'm told it was charming; *I* hardly saw it. I was commuting 150 miles each way to my last year of college.

Since there was no public transportation, I had to have a car. So as a wedding gift, my parents kindly gave us their Ford station wagon. I've never quite been able to break it to them that over the next four years, this gift cost us twenty-eight hundred dollars in repairs.

I'll be the first to admit that no car functions at its best when it has to be parked outside in continuously sub-zero weather in fairly constant blizzards and icestorms. Not to mention that this was a car that had grown up in a milder climate and was used to sleeping in a warm garage. As for its starting average that year, it batted about .200.

By January, every one of its internal organs had failed at least once, a situation aggravated by the local repair shop's singular inability to repair anything completely. They always came up with these incredibly clever ways to resolve the immediate problem, but as I explained to them one day, it was nice to know that the back window could be unstuck by banging on the solenoid with a screwdriver, but I was hoping not to have to do that *every* time.

In their efforts to get the car to function properly, they systematically replaced the thermostat, water pump, valves, and ignition coil, but in spite of these heroics, a service call was invariably needed to get me on the road to school.

Now, I was depending on this vehicle to get me to classes, labs, and exams, and even when the weather was good and the car was working, this was not an uncomplicated or relaxed journey. The entire trip was on one-lane, unplowed country roads, and my departure from home had to be scientifically calculated to get me to Roseboom before the cows crossed and to Route 145 before the Mobil Oil trucks. Who needed a dead battery on top of pressures like that?

By March, both my relationship with cars and the car itself had reached a state of irreparable breakdown. Every time I went even to the supermarket, I had to climb into a snowbank, open the hood, push down on the fan belt and turn the flywheel two spokes counterclockwise, take off the air filter and prop open the choke with a screwdriver, climb out of the snowbank and start her up. (When I said the local repair shop was into creative mechanics, I did not exaggerate.)

By May, I was considering dropping out of college to become a mechanic. At that point in my life, Greek history had far less relevance than carburetor adjustment.

I know it wasn't the car's fault. But since then, with cars and me, it's never been love.

One of our first acts on California soil (after escaping six-bedroom mansions and disposing of psychotic cats, of course) was to buy a brand-new, shiny Vega.

It hurts me deeply to say what I am about to say because, as cars go, I always loved our Vega. As a matter of fact, I am the only person I ever knew who loved or defended a Vega. (Even GM finally got the message and stopped making them.) It was compact, simple, got good mileage.

It also started burning oil at twenty-eight thousand miles.

When it came right down to it, a Vega was probably no worse

than any other car. Name another make of automobile and we have a friend with a Saab story about it. And most of our friends' stories are far worse than ours.

My boss, Marvin, for example, bought a new VW Rabbit, which stopped dead a mile from the dealership. The dealer towed it back and fixed it. This time Marvin got as far as the fast lane of the freeway before it croaked.

The friends with the Saab have already spent two thousand dollars on repairs. They say they can't afford to sell it; at this point, it's an *investment*.

The oil-burning problem, alas, appeared to be epidemic among Vegas. I pulled into our friendly local gas station one day and asked the attendant to check if I needed more oil. "What do you mean, 'if'?" he said.

Actually, I wouldn't be fair if I didn't say that the engine itself hardly needed a repair in three years, which was certainly an improvement over its predecessor. So in that sense, we'd been very pleased with the Vega and almost wouldn't have minded if it had just burned a few gallons of oil here and there.

If only the windshield weren't caving in!

Before the car was two years old, we noticed around the front and back windows that it was rusting through. Pretty soon it was *raining* through.

The local body shops said the windows were improperly sealed at the factory, and they wanted $150 to reseal them, never mind the rust repair. Several levels of GM people couldn't have been more sympathetic about it, but pointed out that the warranty was up, besides which we lived in a "wet" climate. (Southern California? I'd really hate to see a Vega in Seattle.) So we had to ask ourselves, did we want to spend several hundred on a (by this time) oil-burning Vega?

"That's a question?" said Ralph.

The only logical option seemed to be to sell it.

"I think, though, that we've got to be very honest about its shortcomings to prospective buyers," cautioned Ralph. "This is the kind of car that if you aren't, they'll come back and burn down your house."

"What would be an honest ad?" I said thoughtfully.

"How about 'Chevy Vega, low mileage, like old,'" said Ralph drily.

I tried to be philosophical about it. "Well," I said, "cars don't last forever."

"Since when," said Ralph, "is three years forever? I refuse to be a slave to the automotive industry any longer. We're a two-car family. Now we will be a one-car family. I will start taking the bus to work."

The problem with that was that the bus system that served our area was extremely poor. Some days it took Ralph as much as four times longer to get to work. But to his credit, he stuck it out for almost two months. At the end of that time, however, he came home a beaten man.

"They got me," he was muttering under his breath. And continued to mutter all the way to the new-car dealer.

"There are some things," I said to Ralph soothingly, "that are bigger than both of us."

Sickness

When Ralph and I got married, it was my understanding that it was to have and to hold, in sickness and in health, till transfer to Bakersfield.

All those have held except the part about sickness.

If there is a vile virus lurking within three hundred feet, I will get it. But that's not the problem. The problem is that Ralph regards my getting sick as a malicious act.

My susceptibility to illness, unfortunately, is exacerbated by some very kissy friends. ("Louise!" Kiss, slobber. "I've got the most awful news! I have infectious hepatitis!")

Ralph, on the other hand, has hardly had a sick day in his

life. I'm grateful, of course, but a man who has never been sick lacks the proper compassion.

I first learned this during the second year of our marriage when I was in the bathroom being sick and Ralph poked his head in the door and said cheerfully, "Tennis, anyone?" He really did.

The perception of illness in a family member is not within Ralph's visual or auditory capabilities.

Ralph has always subscribed to the Denial School of Medicine: Ignore it and it will go away. When I'm sick, on the other hand, I want a little sympathy. Not that I get it, mind you. Ralph is always just sure I got sick to ruin his good time.

I remember one summer I came back from a visit to New York with some awful illness — a persistent fever, malaise, and abdominal pain.

"It's just a little stomach flu," insisted Ralph. "Just concentrate on mind over matter."

"Who has stomach flu for two weeks?" I said.

Having worked in various medical settings as a secretary and an administrative assistant, my own differential diagnoses included appendicitis, pleurisy, peptic ulcer, acute aseptic peritonitis, cholecystitis, ruptured hernia, incipient colitis, ovarian cysts, and obstruction of the large bowel secondary to a benign tumor.

When I wasn't better after two and a half weeks, I finally realized I had no recourse but to take The Cure. The Cure, as most everyone knows, consists of going to your internist and paying for an expensive office visit and a bunch of exorbitantly priced tests. By some perverse law of human nature, this simple act has been shown to cure 97 percent of ailments, usually even before the test results are back.

Actually, I blame my internist for the fact that The Cure didn't work. So sure was he that it was simply a nondescript virus that all he did was charge me $26.00 for a "medium" office visit (five minutes) and didn't do a single expensive test. Half a Cure, alas, is no cure at all.

So in the next few days, not only did I get sicker, but I developed the worst sore throat I can remember. It took me a full thirty seconds to work up the courage to swallow (and even then I frequently chickened out).

It was when I called Ralph at the office that afternoon and said, "I don't want to alarm you, but I think I may be dead by nightfall," that it became apparent it was time to go back for another consultation. This time the doctor ordered the whole shebang and I fully expected to be at least improved by morning. Instead, two days later, I got a call from him informing me that my throat culture showed beta strep (frankly, I'd had it pegged as diphtheria), and my blood work showed lots of lymphocytes.

"They indicate you have a virus," he explained. I needed him to tell me that? My spleen was pushing on my kneecap. "Also," he continued, "your LDH, SGOT, SGPT, GGTP, and Alk Phos are all elevated."

I wasn't sure what to clutch first. I'd never had an elevated SGOT, etc., and frankly, it sounded serious. I had this sudden image of a good friend of ours — concern, grief, and shock on his stunned face — saying to Ralph, "Ralph . . . I just heard . . . I'm so sorry." And Ralph saying, "We thought she just had a little flu. But then without warning, pffft! — her Alk Phos went. They transfused immediately, of course, but already her LDH, SGOT, and SGPT were involved. It was the GGTP that finally did it."

The doctor's voice interrupted this tragic reverie. "It just means your liver has been affected by the virus. We'll watch it, of course, but I'm sure you'll be fine."

Fortunately, the strep throat at least could be cured with penicillin. And now that my previously unnamed complaints had impressive names and initials, Ralph was much more sympathetic. ("I didn't realize you were *really* sick," he says, after I've just spent three weeks lying there like death warmed over.)

Beautiful was the morning some days later when I woke up

and found I could swallow. Instantly I began planning an exhaustive schedule of events to make up for time lost. Ralph, however, counseled caution. As he pointed out, one swallow doesn't make a summer.

The problem, alas, with strep throats and funny livers is that if you tell your friends you have them, you will certainly get the sympathy due you. But you'll also get to eat with a plastic knife and fork for the next six times you go over there.

Where illness is concerned, there is no justice.

Appliance repair

Hardly a week goes by without some individual (who has to be a man) telling us housewives how lucky we are to have all these modern laborsaving devices our grandmothers didn't have.

And to you, sir, I say, "Horse manure."

I have had a long-standing love-hate relationship with modern appliances. (Love when they work; hate when they don't.) There's nothing that turns me off laborsaving devices like spending a whole day's labor trying to locate a part for one of them.

"Hello, Authorized Dealer?" went the conversation one bright fall morning several years back. "This is Mrs. DeGrave, and my dryer ate its gasket, which is fortunately still under warranty."

"Yes," said the Authorized Dealer, "the two-dollar-and-eighty-nine-cent gasket comes free. But the labor will cost you seventeen fifty."

"You call that a warranty?" I said. "Well, then, can you sell me just the part?"

But he said no, you had to get the authorized labor with the authorized part.

"But," I protested, "a chimpanzee could install this part."

It didn't make good economic sense to spend $17.50 to get a $2.89 part installed, so I sat down and placed some two dozen phone calls over three hours and finally found a parts distributor who didn't have it, but said he would in two weeks.

In two weeks, I call and check and the guy says, "Sure we got it, honey," and I jump into my step-saver car, after first throwing a roast into my laborsaving oven (whose new bake igniter had just cost $51.00 plus a day shot waiting for the repairman), and off I went, sixteen miles to the parts distributor.

"Sorry, sweetheart. Thought I remembered that part coming in, but I guess it didn't. Try me again in a few weeks."

So I went home and called the Authorized Dealer and he said he still had the part, which he still couldn't sell me a la carte, but since my warranty had now expired he would now have to charge me not only the $17.50 authorized labor but also the cost of the part the chimpanzee could have installed, and that the soonest they could come would be three days, if I could guarantee that someone would be home all day Friday.

Well, there it was Friday, and while I, Mrs. Lucky Housewife, was stuck home waiting, I couldn't help but reflect that Grandma's fireplace never needed a fifty-dollar bake igniter, nor her clothesline a new gasket, nor did her icebox leak Freon, nor did her dishpan flood the kitchen, nor did her carpet sweeper explode nor her can opener short out, nor did her washtub blow hoses or her trash can jam up — and there came the repairman.

Now the only thing that needed a new gasket was me.

Pets

After Ralph got out of the Navy and we bought a house of our own, we both felt that we wanted to have a pet again. So we left the house one Sunday morning armed with the classifieds and came home that afternoon with an adorable eight-week-old puppy.

The biggest problem we'd had with pets before was agreeing

on a course of action and then being consistent about it, though of course, we both agreed that we'd improved tremendously since the time we'd gotten our first puppy just after we were married. Ralph was a very strict puppy father then; he allowed pets none of the simple joys of life, like sleeping in our bed or eating off our plates. (I had grown up with a house full of pets; Ralph had never had one of any kind.)

I was a new bride at the time and didn't like arguments. I figured that what Ralph didn't know wouldn't hurt him, and the puppy quickly perceived that as soon as Ralph left the house in the morning, it was a whole new ballgame.

The puppy would join me at the table for breakfast, followed by a nap on Ralph's pillow.

"How come my pillow smells like the dog?" Ralph used to ask. "Every night I have this recurrent dream that he is sleeping on my head."

"Beats me," I said. This was before my assertiveness-training program.

Our new puppy, Alfred, quickly presented us with some problems requiring parental intervention: house training.

After a mature adult discussion, it was decided by the person with the louder voice that Alfred was to reside outside at night until he learned the difference between green grass and green rugs. (I was in favor of just putting newspaper down on the kitchen floor.)

I personally would rather the house had stunk to high heaven than Alfred should be lonely. But in the name of consistency, I agreed with Ralph's plan.

Alfred was placed in the backyard that night (sixty-four degrees) with three blankets, food, milk, a ticking alarm clock wrapped in Ralph's undershirt, and about twenty dollars' worth of chewy toys.

Now, consistency is one thing, but a piteously crying puppy throwing his tiny defenseless body against the back door for three straight nights is another.

Ralph and I didn't get any sleep, partly because of the

crying, and mostly because we were fighting about whether or not to let him in. Ralph-with-the-rocklike-heart was against it.

"Alfred is not spending the night in the house until he stops making doody in my closet," said Ralph emphatically.

"Look, Ralph," I said, representing the compassion of womankind, "dogs are people too. He wants love and companionship."

"I think I'm changing my mind about all this," said Ralph, who after three sleepless nights looked like death warmed over.

"You mean you think we should let him in?" I said.

"No," said Ralph. "But I'd consider sending Alfred to a foster home."

Fortunately, however, we all managed to accustom ourselves to this new situation — Alfred to sleeping outside, Ralph to getting a full night's sleep again, and me to the fact that I was married to a man who could be an unfeeling brute. And as puppies are wont to do, Alfred gradually became housebroken, and less gradually stopped eating everything in sight, including shoes, books, pantyhose, and ties. On one occasion, he even ate a whole tube of rubber cement and went around for three weeks afterward with one ear glued to the top of his head.

We loved Alfred. He was cute and terribly affectionate, and very much the baby that we didn't have. Where else could you get so much adoration for so little effort?

Finding a place to stash Alfred when we went out of town, however, turned out to be a chronic problem for Ralph and me. Alfred absolutely hated kennels, and if we left him in the backyard over night, he got lonely and barked his head off, such that the neighbors were plotting violent acts toward us by the time we returned.

I figured there must be at least one other person in this predicament, so I placed an ad in the classifieds. "Want to exchange pet-sitting 2–3 times per year with owner of small dog. Prefer other animal lover with fenced yard."

Now, Ralph said afterward that it was my own fault for

placing the ad in the Personals, where it ended up sandwiched between "Male with depth, sensitivity, intelligence . . ." and "Mary—It's OK. We know. Come home." Ralph claims that there is something about the Personals that brings the fringe element crawling out of the woodwork.

Actually, none of the calls I got could be classified as kinky, but I got several that absolutely tore the heartstrings. My theory is that the responses had nothing to do with it being in the Personals; it was the words "animal lover" that got me into trouble. Unwittingly, I set myself up as a social-service agency for pet-related problems.

All these people called me up in desperate circumstances, like they were going to be out of town for ten weeks or four months and they couldn't bear that little Fido, a very sensitive animal, should languish in a kennel for such a long time, and since I was an animal lover . . .

Or the lady whose husband was going to be in the hospital forever and she absolutely had to get a job to support herself but she couldn't bring herself to do it until she'd found adequate care from 3:00 to 11:00 P.M. daily for her little dog, whom she couldn't bear to leave alone, and she couldn't pay me, what with the medical bills, but she wondered if perhaps a fellow animal lover . . .

Then there was the couple who sounded almost perfect (it didn't bother me that the dog had glaucoma and needed eyedrops several times daily; I could do it) until it came out that the deal would also include nine cats. And what could I say to the dear little old woman who desperately wanted to visit her ailing sister but couldn't find *anyplace* that would take her twelve-year-old fox terrier who had seizures and was incontinent and "bites, but not as often as he used to"?

The problem was that I *am* an animal lover and I couldn't bear that Fido should languish in a kennel for four months either. Desperation knows no bounds; one lady called and said, "You specified a small dog. Would an Afghan be too big?"

Fortunately, the outcome of all this was that I did finally make an exchange arrangement with the owners of a dachshund and a cockapoo.

"Alfred," I said to the dog after the cockapoo and his owner had left, "I hope you appreciate what your mommy is trying to do for you."

Alfred, however, just rolled over and went to sleep.

Dogs may make good companions. But they're lousy on gratitude.

Stress (or, A womb of one's own)

My prescription for dealing with life's stresses is to go back to the womb.

Wombing, of course, is simply a variation on your basic hot shower. The best way to womb, I've found, is to make the bathroom as dark as possible, curl up like a pretzel on the floor of the shower stall, and just let the hot water pour over you. Close your eyes. Let your mind go. Make funny noises. Feel warm and safe. Remember the good old days.

There is no stress on me that cannot be temporarily relieved in this manner. I make all my important decisions in the womb.

Ralph has never understood what makes it so effective, but he is very good about it. He has never disturbed me in the womb, except the time the house was on fire.

"It's like being reborn," I used to explain to him. With the stresses on me at the time, I found I needed to be reborn about once a day. Fortunately, it was inexpensive. The only other cost besides the hot water was a gallon of dry-skin lotion.

The length of time you can spend in the womb is dependent only on the size of your hot-water heater. In the first house we rented in San Diego, the hot-water heater was only five gallons, so there were no opportunities for me to do my womb routine there. (The best I could be was a three-minute egg.)

"Psychoanalysts have long said that regression is a part of the creative process," I told Ralph. "It unleashes my creative energies."

"Is it possible you could tie them up briefly and make dinner?" said Ralph.

Which brings me to my next point. Wombing is not for everyone. Ralph, for example, is not a womber at all. He much prefers to relax in a regular bath in a well-lighted room with a socially relevant novel and his rubber duck.

"Wombing is just very relaxing and therapeutic," I tried explaining one last time. "I go in there where it's warm and dark and wet and I thrive."

"You and mold," sighed Ralph.

I keep trying. But so far, I've never been able to get Ralph to see the dark.

Inflation

If I didn't know before, I now know what inflation is.

Inflation is a bill for $45.00 to have a $2.89 rubber gasket installed on your dryer.

Anyone knows that $17.50 plus $2.89 comes to $20.39. So how was it that I got a bill for $45.00? I was curious about that too.

"Hello, Authorized Dealer?" I said optimistically. "Your computer has made a terrible mistake."

He looked up my records. "You're right," he said. "The bill is incorrect."

I breathed a sigh of relief; there wasn't going to be any fight about it. Even they could see at a glance that $45.00 for a lousy gasket job was way out of line. Even $17.50 was ridiculous.

"Let me recalculate for you," he said. "The problem was that our rates went up a week after your job was done and your bill was accidentally computed under the new rates. Let's see, that would still be two eighty-nine for the part, but only twenty-eight fifty for the labor."

"Twenty-eight fifty!" I said. "They told me a service call was seventeen fifty."

"It is," he said. "For the first fifteen minutes."

"They never told me that!" I said. "How long did that turkey claim he was at my house?"

"Thirty-six minutes."

"No wonder he was so slow and friendly," I said. "If I'd known he was charging by the minute, I'd have stood over him with a whip and with orders not to take his eyes off my dryer. Twenty-eight fifty is absolutely outrageous for that job! All he had to do was slap a little glue on it and stick it on."

"Gee," said the Authorized Dealer, sounding almost wounded, "I thought you'd be happy you got in under the old rates."

"Let me get this straight," I said. "If I'd had this same job done one week later, it would have cost me forty-five dollars?"

"Correct."

"That's not outrageous. It's immoral."

"That's what it costs to send a man out, lady."

"My *lawyer* doesn't charge that much."

"Then get your lawyer out to fix your dryer."

"Forty-five dollars!" I said. "God forbid something was actually *wrong* with the machine. I might have had to put up my house as collateral."

"For the future, maybe you want to purchase a service contract, thirty-four fifty. We could just add it to your bill."

"Twenty-eight fifty, forty-five dollars, thirty-four fifty . . ." I mumbled under my breath.

On my tombstone, it's going to say, "All she wanted was a three-dollar gasket. And a chance."

In-laws: The first visit

Ralph came home from work one night and announced that his parents weren't going to live forever and he wanted to express his gratitude. (For their dedication, not for their dying.) So he dipped into our savings and sent them airfare to come visit, plus a ticket for the dog whom they wouldn't come without.

This was to be Mom and Pop's first airline flight and we were praying everything would go smoothly. Large metropolitan airports can be confusing even to the most experienced of travelers, and there was no doubt in our minds that Pop would be too proud to ask certain key questions like, "Where is Delta?"

"Please," we pleaded with them before they left, "you have only forty-five minutes to change planes. Don't be afraid to ask for help."

"Eh," said Pop. "Not necessary."

As it turned out, Mom and Pop did fine. A kindly stewardess took one look at them and personally escorted them to their next plane. Due to delays, the airline offered the passengers free champagne, and Mom, not one to pass up a bargain even though a nondrinker, had five glasses and got off the plane absolutely snockered, exalting the virtues of Delta.

Ralph and I wanted this to be a special visit and had planned a full schedule of activities, including an extensive sight-seeing tour, concert, movies, a little party to meet our friends, and meals at several restaurants.

Now, there were two things Ralph and I promised each other about this visit. The first was that we weren't going to make ourselves crazy trying to please Pop. Actually, it's not that Pop can't be pleased; he just won't *admit* it. You could give him a million dollars and say, "Well, Pop, how do you like *that?*" and all you'd get would be a shrug and one of three stock responses: "Eh," "Nothing special," or "We've got the same thing in Florida."

"Ralph," I said every morning of the visit, "we must face the fact that Pop is never going to say 'Wowie, gee, terrific!' Pop is just not your wowie, gee, terrific sort of person. We must accept this. We have planned very nice activities for today. We know they are nice. So we will not ask Pop his opinion of them."

"Agreed," said Ralph with equal resolve.

And after every activity, we turned to Pop and said eagerly, "Well, Pop, how did you like it?" And Pop shrugged and said, "Eh."

The second thing we promised ourselves was that we were not going to try to control what Mom said to other people. We just decided that she was Ralph's mother and we were proud of her no matter what she said. And she had a right to say anything she wanted.

It's just that Mom has a heart of gold and tries to help your career in ways that set you back ten years. In an effort to give a little hand to my budding new writing career, for example, she told the editor of the local paper how nice it was of him to print my articles and not charge me anything. She then exhorted him to be patient, as the family felt I was bound to improve over the years.

The other reason we decided not to try to control Mom is that there *is* no controlling Mom. Ralph did try once during the visit, despite his resolve. Mom was overwhelmed with delight that Ralph had cared enough about her to send her airfare to come visit, and she wanted that fact known.

"Mom," said Ralph at one point, "I'm going to introduce you to some friends, and would you please stop referring to me as your son, the millionaire?" Mom reluctantly agreed.

"Pleased to meet you," she said instead. "So you're a friend of my son Ralph, who sent us six hundred and thirty-one dollars to come out here."

On the last day of the visit, we put them on the plane back home, Mom and Pop and the dog (who reportedly had a wonderful time). At the airport Mom cried and said it had been the trip of a lifetime. Even Pop was a little teary-eyed. We got teary-eyed seeing them so teary-eyed.

Then we came home and slept for five hours. It's exhausting work being a grateful son.

Five (tragic) laws of sex, anatomy, and civilization

Tragic law of sex #1: Frequency. No matter how much you enjoy sex, the odds that both of you will consistently, over a long period of time, want to have sex (a) at the same time and (b) with the same frequency are (c) slim. At some point, it is likely that one of you will be accused of being frigid/fragile/unimaginative/repressive/overly emotional/withholding/too sensitive/preoccupied with hygiene, which certainly isn't true. The other will be accused of being insatiable/rough/overly imaginative/bestial/unfeeling/self-centered/goal oriented/unconcerned about hygiene, which may not be true either. Oddly, the incidence of these accusations seems to occur in direct proportion to how pressured, provocative, and grouchy one or the other of you has been feeling, and in inverse proportion to the number of times you've gone roller skating together lately.

Tragic law of sex and civilization #2: Civilization has given mankind many improvements. Women's sex lives have not been one of them. Just when women finally got social permission to have orgasm, and stopped caring whether it was vaginal or clitoral, someone brought up single versus multiple. This is progress?

Cardinal rule of marriage #3: Never withhold sex to get back at your spouse for real or imagined grievances. Not only does this set a dangerous precedent and risk complicating the sexual relationship, but threatening to write pornography under his mother's maiden name is far more effective.

Law of unequal anatomy #4: The Bible says women will give birth in sorrow. What it doesn't say is that they will also stand in long lines outside the ladies' restroom during intermission at the theater. Intellectually, all men (sic) are created equal.

Anatomically, women were not created equal to men. This is pathetically obvious at a picnic.

Tragic law of civilization #5: Myths. It is obvious from movies, paperback novels, and TV commercials that everyone else has a more dramatic sex life than you:

She is multiorgasmic. He did it seven times in one night and would have done it an eighth except that the casts on his legs from his recent motorcycle-stunt accident were bothering him. Both sleep all night passionately entwined in each other's arms without cutting off anyone's circulation. In the morning, they reflexively reach for each other again, though still in REM sleep. He uses Brut; she uses scented hygiene products.

Gradually, as you get a little older, it finally dawns on you that a sure way to ruin your good time — sexually and otherwise — is to confuse movies, paperback novels, and TV commercials with reality. Your spouse is really pretty sexy. You're not bad either. Here you've been wasting your energy comparing your life to Harold Robbins and Close-up commercials.

So long, Frederick's of Hollywood!

Money

There are people who have told me they could never be close to someone whose checkbook balanced to the penny. Actually, mine doesn't always balance to the penny. I've gotten looser as I get older. If it's within a dime, I just let it go.

Actually, the reason for this is that for the first five years of our marriage, Ralph and I frequently lived in rather tenuous financial circumstances. There were months when we were withdrawing the last ten dollars out of our savings account a dollar at a time. So I got in the habit of watching our cash flow down to the penny, and now I just like to do it. This, by the way, demonstrates Allport's Theory of the Functional

Autonomy of Motives. (You have no idea how long I've waited to use that.)

I remember when we first got married, Ralph and I thought how romantic *and* practical it would be if we could someday work together professionally. The way we figured it, Ralph would be the brains of the outfit because of his advanced degree, and I'd be the business manager, since, despite Ralph's advanced training, he cannot balance a checkbook.

I'm serious. Briefly, in Colorado, Ralph insisted on taking over management of our finances. The only way we ever got the mess of our checking account cleared up was to close the account and move out of state.

Ralph's approach to managing a checkbook can best be described as "magical." He was always just *sure* he'd remember to record the check later (only overly compulsive, anal-retentive neurotics like his wife insisted on recording the amount of the check when it was written; what, after all, did God give you a memory for?) and maintained an unwavering childlike faith that we had a sufficient balance to cover it.

Part of the problem, of course, was that the money to pay our bills was invariably hanging out in our savings account, not in the checking, where it was needed. I should mention here that right about the time Ralph took over the checkbook, there broke out in our area a long and vicious battle among banks that was to change the course of financial history. It was called the Great Savings and Loan Crock-pot War, and Ralph saw a lot of action.

The savings and loans in our area were engaged in fierce competition to attract new accounts, and new deposits to old accounts, offering such enticements as cheese boards, baked-bean crocks, gravy boats, and even watches. It was cutthroat. The larger the deposit, the nicer the gift. There was no minimum time the deposit had to stay there, and no limit to the number of gifts. You can begin to see the possibilities.

The prospect of all those free Crock-pots and cheese boards

drove Ralph into a frenzy. He was like a man possessed. As soon as either of us got a paycheck, he would promptly deposit the entire amount into our savings and collect a cheese board. The next week, because we needed the money to pay our bills, he would withdraw the money from the savings and deposit it into our checking.

Now, this could have gone on indefinitely, except for two things. One day Ralph accidentally lost our savings passbook right after depositing our entire month's earnings. (He'd held off paying our bills for thirty days so he'd have a large enough deposit for a percolator.) This not only froze our account for ten days (I'm sure at that point the bank would have liked to freeze it for ten years), but left us exactly $7.70 in our checking account to live on in the interim. I was furious.

The second was that the savings and loan made a sudden policy change. Now, I wasn't privy to that board meeting, but I can well imagine the dialogue that occurred there: "Ladies and Gentlemen of the Board, it has come to our attention that one of our depositors will soon have a corner on the cheese-board/gravy-boat market, not to mention a dangerous stockpile of baked-bean crocks. This on an account which last year accrued interest of nine dollars. There are times in the course of history when drastic action must be taken to avert disaster. From now on, One Gift Per Account Per Year."

Ralph, of course, was crushed when they told him. (He had satisfied this year's Christmas list by June and was already working on next year's.) That took all the fun out of it for Ralph, who freely admitted that some of the finer points of financial management, like paying our bills, were frankly boring to him. Regardless of commonly assigned roles, he concluded, whichever one of us displayed the greater talent for doing the income tax and handling money should do it. And "whichever one" has been me ever since.

Family Planning, Part 1: Adoption

The decision of a couple to add a third party to their relationship is a monumental one. When that wish is frustrated by the inability to produce a child, both partners may experience feelings ranging from disappointment to severe depression.

For couples who decide to adopt, the process of waiting for and then finally receiving a child is especially difficult since there is no set, structured time frame. Also, the attachment that builds in normal pregnancy — the baby's kicking, the enormous bodily changes, the drama of the birth — is not available to the adoptive mother. The situation is further exacerbated by the dwindling numbers of infants available for adoption, which frequently results in a wait of several years.

That's a long time.

Twenty-six interesting reasons to have a baby

Whenever anyone used to ask me why I wanted to have a baby, I always said, "To get one of Mrs. Nilsson's coffee cakes."

That wasn't the real reason, of course, but it had the decided advantage that no one ever inquired further.

Anna Nilsson, you see, promised us one of her coffee cakes when we became parents. Anna is a wonderful little old Swedish lady who lives down the street and makes a coffee cake the prospect of which leaves Ralph and me salivating like Pavlov's dogs. (As a masseuse, she once gave Johnny Weissmuller a massage, but that's immaterial.)

The whole business about Mrs. Nilsson's coffee cake started one day when my friend Gina asked me, "Why do you want to have a baby?"

It's weird. All your life you just know you want to be a parent, then somebody asks you why and you don't have an answer. So I said, "To get one of Mrs. Nilsson's coffee cakes."

"To tell you the truth," said Gina, "the reason I'm asking is that somebody asked me the other day and I didn't know either."

"It *is* a little different with our generation," I said. "It's not like you've just homesteaded Oklahoma and need a few extra pairs of hands in the south pasture, or that half the Western Hemisphere has just been wiped out by bubonic plague."

"Of course," said Gina, "there's always reasons like it would make your parents ecstatic, or because all your friends have kids, or it's just instinctive, or we've just been conditioned to be mothers. Maybe even to prove our femininity or because we're afraid we might be sorry later if we don't."

"Yes," I said, "but are we going to admit to any of those?"

"Not on your life," said Gina.

"You could have a baby so you'd have someone to take care of you in your old age or to alleviate your fear of dying," I suggested.

"I'm twenty-four years old," said Gina. "Who's going to grow old?"

"And I guess some people have kids so they can redo the mistakes their own parents made," I said.

"Liver," said Gina emphatically. "My kids are never going to have to eat liver."

"I guess I keep thinking I should be having kids for some really altruistic reason," I said. "Like, with the population explosion, you shouldn't have a kid just because you *want* one."

"I know what you mean," said Gina. "Sometimes I say to myself that I'd like to be a parent so I could help a unique individual grow up and develop and become his or her own person."

"That's beautiful," I said.

"At times I even believe it," said Gina glumly. "But you're adopting an infant, Louise, so you've already got a really noble reason. You're opening your heart and home to a poor unwanted waif."

"Gina," I said, "there's a minimum three-year waiting list for those poor unwanted waifs."

"You know," said Gina, "I don't think it's unfair to say that we would each have a lot to give as parents. The kid could do worse."

"True," I said. "Basically, I think what I want from a baby is to love it and hope it loves me back. Do you think that's a good enough reason by itself?"

"I don't know," said Gina. "The only thing I'm sure of is that I want a baby."

"Yeah," I said. "And maybe we'll never know all the reasons why."

"Now that we've come up with all these different reasons," said Gina, "what are you going to say if someone asks you?"

I thought for a moment. "To get one of Mrs. Nilsson's coffee cakes," I said.

Emily Post's guide to announcing your infertility

Applying for adoption can bring up all sorts of sensitive issues for those of us in the infertility set.

Ralph and I, for example, had been reading letters in Ann Landers' column for years from childless couples who complained that the world was full of thoughtless boors who had the gall to ask them whose "fault" it was.

At the time we applied for adoption we were feeling very

sensitive about it all, especially since a recent study had shown that I was the only woman in the Western Hemisphere who wasn't pregnant. So before we told anyone, we sat down and thought up a list of absolutely vicious rejoinders for insensitive questions.

But nobody asked. This began to bother me.

"Ralph," I said finally, "no one has ever asked us whose fault it is. Are we that outside the mainstream of American life?"

"I don't know," said Ralph, "but lately no one would have to ask. You tell them."

"I do not."

"Well, you give them broad hints. Like whenever anyone tells you what a fertile mind you have, you say, 'I'm glad *some* part of me is.' And when Mike told you not to take pictures right into the sun because it would make you blind and sterile, you looked up from your camera without your glasses and said, 'That's OK. I'm already both.' And then . . ."

Anyway, despite our anxieties, we finally decided that it was simply easier to tell people we were adopting than to face another three years of cocktail party dialogue like:

"Do you have children?"

"No."

"How many years have you been married?"

"Six."

"Oh." (Pause.) "My niece, she takes fertility pills . . ."

Of course, one of the most difficult things adoptive parents face is the loss of narcissistic gratification in producing little miniatures of themselves, not to mention the truly staggering grief (and it really is grief) that the child who has lived so long in your minds will never be. Ralph and I did a lot of not-so-successful rationalizing to deal with this.

"When you think about it, Ralph," I would say, "are our genes really so great? What if the kid turned out to have both of our worst features?"

"Your teeth and my nose," reflected Ralph. "You're right, it wouldn't be fair. Let's adopt."

During our long wait on the agency's list, we were actually very pleasantly surprised at most people's sensitivity about it.

One afternoon, however, I was in a baby department at a large store and explained to the saleswoman that I wasn't sure of sizes because we were waiting to adopt a baby who might be as old as seven or eight months. And she went on for ten minutes about how adoption just wasn't such a *stigma* anymore and that I shouldn't feel *inadequate* or *any* less of a woman.

I know it's a difficult thing for people to handle. But I just kept wishing she'd ask me whose fault it was. . . .

The adoption wait

One year, one month

After we'd been on the waiting list a little over a year, Ralph and I took a required child-care class that taught the ins of feeding and outs of diaper changing, and all the nitty-gritty practical stuff in between. It was a special course just for adoptive parents (so we wouldn't get depressed about not having postpartum depressions).

I was actually surprised at how interested Ralph seemed to be in the course. He even went alone one week when I was out of town. I was delighted, of course, but also curious as to what motivated him to go.

"Fear," he said without hesitation. "I suddenly started thinking how much we know about infant care. I also got to wondering whether this is why babies as a group have never liked us."

This, alas, was true. My whole life, whenever I picked up a baby, it cried. Even if it had just had a bottle or had just been changed or was in a coma, it cried. This is not conducive to confidence as a mother.

I began to develop this theory that maybe babies have some built-in survival mechanism that can sense when the person picking them up is really nervous about it. As if something deep inside of them says, "I think this broad is going to drop me on my head. *Waaaaahhhhhh.*"

The class was invaluable in giving us confidence, and we both very much liked the teacher, who was an adoptive mother herself. She did, however, have this incredible tendency toward Freudian slips, which, depending on how you took them, could add all sorts of moral questions about which baby furnishings to buy.

"One thing about a playpen," she explained, for example, "is that it teaches the child to play with himself."

The teacher also emphasized that now was the time to throw away any old prescription drugs in the medicine cabinet, as we might be so busy when the baby came that we'd forget about it. Although we did it for the baby's safety, it actually turned out to be kind of fun. There's nothing like sitting on the edge of the bathroom sink reminiscing about your more dramatic former illnesses while clutching the very vial of pills that probably saved your life, or at least relieved your nasal congestion.

"What should we do about this one?" said Ralph, holding up a small bottle.

"Don't throw it out yet," I said, "but put it out of the baby's reach." (Our rotten luck, the *kid* would get pregnant.)

On the last night of class, we were awarded little cards making us certified parents. This assuaged a certain anxiety for us.

"Now, if the kid turns out to be a deadbeat," I said to Ralph, "it won't be *our* fault."

And every morning after that, Ralph woke me up in the morning going *Waaaahhhhhhh* in my ear. So I could get used to the sound.

One year, six months

These are touchy times to be a mother.

Since we had been waiting a year and a half for a baby and

hoped to be adoptive parents soon, I asked two friends who were over visiting one evening about playpens and diapers and things. Innocent questions, yes?

LOUISE So what's the story on playpens? A couple of people said I shouldn't get one.

JANICE I would *never* put *my* child in a cage!

LOUISE Oh, well, I just —

CHARLOTTE Bull. It's not a cage. It's for the kid's own protection.

JANICE It's not so hard to childproof your house and let him crawl around. That way you don't inhibit creative exploration.

CHARLOTTE Creative what? Are you out of your skull? You can never childproof a house so that a baby can't find something dangerous to get into.

JANICE Well, you watch him, of course, you idiot.

LOUISE *(sensing tension)* Moving right along, what about diapers?

CHARLOTTE Life is short. Use a diaper service.

JANICE It's ridiculously expensive. There's no reason anyone with a washer and dryer can't do her own.

CHARLOTTE But why, when the service is so much more convenient?

JANICE Well, if motherhood is such a big inconvenience for some people, I'm not sure why they chose to be mothers.

LOUISE Would anyone like some cookies?

CHARLOTTE Well, I see no sense in other people being complete martyrs about it and making life harder than it has to be.

LOUISE Coffee?

JANICE I'm just saying that some mothers these days don't want to take responsibility for being mothers. For example, I can't understand how some women who don't need to work can leave a small baby with a sitter eight hours a day.

LOUISE Iced tea?

CHARLOTTE It's the quality of the time, not the quantity. Half the women I know who stay home are chronically depressed.

JANICE Well, at least their kids know who their mother is!

LOUISE A diet soda maybe?

CHARLOTTE Well, I happen to believe that a woman who really enjoys working is a better mother than some compulsive neurotic who refuses to let the kid out of her sight.

JANICE *(giving Charlotte a look that would sink Australia)* Well, Louise, what are *you* planning to do when the baby comes?

LOUISE I'm still not sure about working. But I think I'd like to use disposable diapers.

JANICE *(to Charlotte)* Is she for real?

CHARLOTTE What a waste of paper.

One year, ten months

At the open house we went to early in the New Year, several guests were talking about the toys they had bought their children for Christmas. Since we were prospective parents, this was a topic of some interest to Ralph and me.

The general complaint was that the parents had wanted to buy their kids educational toys but the kids wanted the ones they saw advertised on TV.

It all started when the guy on my right turned to the pediatrician who had just joined the group and said, "My wife and I think Baby Alive has anorexia nervosa. She won't eat a thing."

It turned out that the pediatrician and his wife had bought their child a Baby Alive who developed similar complaints. The doll was taken back to the toy store where it was discovered that it was suffering from pyloric stenosis secondary to the pediatrician's daughter trying to feed Baby Alive peanut butter instead of her special formula.

"What do you feed her?" I asked with some interest.

"Baby Alive food," said the pediatrician's wife with the most defeated look I have ever seen on a person. She said she always picked up a new supply of it whenever she was down getting another load of Baby Alive's special disposable diapers.

Another party guest told us about a doll that crawled away on the floor by itself. Unfortunately, you had to be a technical genius to get the arms and legs and head positioned exactly right, otherwise the doll just lay there having convulsions.

"You think you've got problems," said another woman. "We got our daughter the Growing Up Skipper doll that grows breasts when you twist her arm. *Twist her arm?*"

The group then began conjecturing what toymakers might come out with in the future in the way of "real" dolls. The general consensus was that now that they had the elimination functions down cold, the next logical step would be to develop dolls with real live medical problems.

Baby Allergy, for example, could have eczema, colic, and mild asthma, and come with milk substitutes, a small pharmacy of expensive medication, and a vial of Valium for her mother.

In tune with the trend to make parents continue to pay out even after the doll has been purchased, someone suggested a doll for the older child called Growing Up Krazie who has multiple neuroses requiring psychotherapy at fifteen bucks a shot. Somebody else suggested that as an offshoot of the popular show about paramedics, there could be a Betty Croaker doll who needed frequent resuscitation.

All this served to make Ralph and me very anxious.

"Promise me now, Ralph," I said as we drove home. "Promise me. Our kid isn't getting anything more complicated than a little red wagon."

Two years, two months

We had originally decided not to change the house around or set up a crib until the adoption people called and said they had a baby for us. Even then — because we were a little superstitious — we weren't going to do anything until we'd gone down for the required meeting to look him (or her) over. (With adoption, you get the kid on approval. Not that we know anyone who's ever sent one back.)

Despite our resolve, we said to ourselves, it's been over two years since we've been waiting, and maybe it's time to get organized. An afternoon's work, yes?

I guess part of the problem was that we had too many choices about where to put the baby because we had such an unconventional floorplan. It was so unconventional we even had to sign papers when we bought the place that we were aware it was set up a little weirdly, though how they thought we could have missed it, I don't know. (In how many other homes is the only access to the master bedroom through the laundry room?)

Well, we decided to put the baby in our room (least street noise), so we moved into the master bedroom (originally the garage), which we'd always used as a guest room because when they delivered the convertible sofa/guest bed, that was the only room except the dining room it would go into. (Always measure carefully.) So the convertible sofa had to go into the dining room (probably meant as a family room?), forcing the dining-room table into what was probably originally intended as the dining alcove (but who knew anymore in this house?), which was currently occupied by Ralph's baby grand piano (he used to play semiprofessionally), forcing the piano into the living room, where we had never put it before because the living room was so small. We moved the piano six times before finding the least bad place for it, but which, no matter where we put it, forced out the living-room sofa, which had to go into the master bedroom with us. (Getting it over the washing machine was hell.)

The piano, alas, now consumed nine-tenths of the living room, such that if you really pushed it, you could now seat a total of three persons, one of them on the piano bench.

We were naturally quite glad we didn't wait until the night before to do all that. This way we had time to get our hernias repaired and all.

Finally we got everything where it was supposed to be, took the crib out of its box and assembled it, and attached the mobile. (Everyone had told us the kid would grow up to be a cretin without a mobile.)

And Ralph wound up the mobile, which played "Farmer in the Dell," and we stepped back to look, and suddenly it hit us.

"Ralph," I said. "That is a crib. It is in our house."

"I wonder what it's doing there," said Ralph.

"You don't suppose," I said, "that maybe we're really getting a baby . . . ? That it isn't all a figment of our imaginations . . . ?"

Of course, within three months we had to get a new mobile. We wore out the first one.

Two years, six months

Probably the most important quality you need to have as a prospective adoptive parent is a tolerance for long-term vagueness.

I didn't have it.

For example, every time I called our adoption worker for a progress report, we had the same conversation:

LOUISE *(friendly and casual)* How are we doing on the list?
WORKER *(also friendly and casual)* OK.
LOUISE I know it's difficult to pinpoint exactly when we'll get our baby . . . *(Maybe we haven't gotten one because you don't like us?)*
WORKER I'm sorry, we really can't predict.
LOUISE Oh, I know, but is it at all possible it could be, say, within the next six months? *(Maybe you're mad because I work?)*
WORKER It's really hard to tell.
LOUISE Well, um, do you think it's likely to be, say, within a year? *(Maybe you're secretly opposed to interreligious marriages?)*
WORKER We just can't say.
LOUISE Within two years? We should have a baby within two years, right? *(Maybe you just can't find a match for us?)*
WORKER We really can't make any promises.

After a while, I began to notice that this difficulty in tolerating vagueness sometimes caused me to operate on a different level.

"Hey," said Ralph one night, "did you call the adoption people today? It's been six months since we talked to them, so they *must* have something more definite to say."

"As a matter of fact," I said happily, "I called and it looks like we might get a baby soon."

"You're kidding!" said Ralph jubilantly, picking me up and whirling me around. "They said that?"

"Oh, no," I said. "They were their usual vague selves."

Ralph dropped me on the floor. "Then why do you think it might be soon?"

"Well," I said, "there was a new quality to their vagueness. More optimistic." Ralph was looking at me as if I were crazy. "It's hard to explain."

"Try," said Ralph drily.

I thought for a moment. "Well, for one, she didn't sigh," I said. "Now, that's new. Oh, and she returned the call after only one message."

"What's that got to do with it?" said Ralph.

"Think about it," I said. "Nobody wants to call back when all they're going to have for you in the foreseeable future is bad news. But if they know they're going to have good news fairly soon . . ."

"That's possible," conceded Ralph. "But is that all?"

"Well," I said, "I think there may have been a tiny twinkle in her voice."

"Tiny *twinkle?*" said Ralph skeptically.

"Next time," I said, "I'm going to let *you* call!"

Then he'd know a tiny twinkle when he heard one.

Two years, nine months

I think the rottenest part of waiting for an adoption is that you have too much choice about parenthood for too long.

About the time that Ralph and I had been gestating on the adoption waiting list for two and three-quarters years, I came to the conclusion that God had the right idea about conception: You got pregnant and you were stuck. Then you had nine months to get used to the idea.

Oh, there was abortion and all if you were really opposed, but for the most part, it was a fait accompli. You couldn't just pick up the phone and cancel out as adoptive parents could.

Now, there was nothing inherently wrong with having a choice right up to the last minute. It was just that I had come to believe by that time that motherhood was not something anyone should dwell on too long, because there was only one conclusion you could come to:

Who needs it?

I don't know whether it was the interminable wait for the baby, the recent offer of some exciting (but alas, full-time) career possibilities for me, or a few experiences with friends' children that began to make parenthood look like an act of heroism. Probably a combination. But for several weeks, I had a severe attack of less-than-enthusiastic feelings about being a mother.

Ralph tried to help me work it out.

"I think it's natural for a prospective mother to be ambivalent," Ralph insisted.

"Who's ambivalent?" I said at the time. "There is no doubt in my mind. I'm *negative*. Let them keep their crummy kid."

It was really getting serious. One morning a casual friend came bounding eagerly up to me on the street to inquire if we had any more news about the baby. "You must be getting *so* excited!" she said.

"No," I said, and walked away.

In my defense, I have to say that it was a rotten thing for the adoption people to have said "any time after the first of the year."

"Maybe we should have asked *what* year," I said morosely to

Ralph one morning. "For six months we have been waking up every morning with the knowledge that we may be parents by nightfall. This is any way to live?"

Even Ralph was getting a little worn down by it all.

"Maybe we'll just have to go the expensive route to get a baby," he sighed.

"You mean a private adoption?" I said.

"No," said Ralph. "Planning a trip to Europe with a large, nonrefundable deposit."

"I don't know, Ralph," I said. "Sometimes I'm ready to forget the whole thing. Look at what a carefree, happy-go-lucky duo we are. Do we know one parent of a child under two who is happy-go-lucky? Or even well rested? And that job at the hospital sounds awfully good."

Then the fateful words crept in. The choice. "It's not too late, you know."

But for some reason (and for several weeks, that reason eluded me), we never canceled. We just waited.

You knew it had been a long time when your crib was dusty.

Three years, forty-two days

From my diary:

It's a boy! Seven pounds eleven ounces!

Actually, the little cutie arrived nearly a month ago but I haven't had a chance to write about him before. (Last week my goal was to take a shower.)

I hope no one will think I am biased when I say that Alan is one of the cutest babies in the Western Hemisphere. I know mothers are not exactly known for their objectivity in these matters, but people who have no reason to lie (his grandfather, aunt, uncle) agree wholeheartedly.

Alan is also alert, responsive, and wonderfully cuddly. Also eats like a horse. Really, I've never seen a kid pack away a bottle with such gusto. (Already he takes six ounces, but Ralph says if you wrang out his T-shirt, you'd get half of that back.)

As may be obvious by now, this kid has won the hearts of the household. This is not to say that his arrival has not been an adjustment. (That may be one of the biggest understatements I ever write.) One day I had this nice placid existence, and twenty-four hours later, I've got this bottomless pit who demands to be fed every two to three hours around the clock.

That first week, I thought I would die.

"We *asked* for this?" I said tearfully to Ralph. I mean, every two to three hours comes around every two to three hours, and I have never been your night-owl sort of person. (That may be another of the biggest understatements I ever write.)

Worse yet, everybody kept saying, "You must be so happy!" Well, a lot of me really *was* so happy. The other part, however, kept wishing I'd get hit by a truck.

It wasn't until the end of the first week that I realized how much my feelings had to do with sheer exhaustion. And unpreparedness. Since we didn't know how old the baby would be, we only had equipment for an older baby. You could have put four Alans into the stretch suits I had for him.

Ralph had been helping a lot, but I was still doing most of the night feedings, and by the seventh day, I was a basket case. So that night, Ralph magnanimously did all the night feedings. The next morning, I was Miss Congeniality and *Ralph* was a basket case. It was then that I first realized there was hope.

The other part of it was, everything takes so much longer when you don't know what you're doing. The first time we tried to transfer him from one of us to the other was a major transaction. ("You got the head?" "Yeah, I got the head, you got the tush?" "OK, I'll ease over the left leg and you . . .")

We got the wrong nipples for the right bottles, sterilized stuff until it practically melted, and learned only belatedly that our experience changing a friend's baby girl did not have total carryover to a baby boy. (Right between the eyes at 2:00 A.M.)

If there was one thing we realized that first week, it was that our training had been all wrong. We didn't need courses in baby care; we needed some in mechanical engineering: Introduction to Assorted Carriers; Rigging the Car Seat 210; Navigation of the Stroller Down Escalators and Up Steps 320.

But after the first week, everything started to get dramatically better. I'm still not sure why, but it did. One night I was feeding him around 3:00 A.M. and wondering if I'd ever have a full night's sleep again. And I looked down at little Alan happily guzzling his bottle, and Alan looked back up at me, and all of a sudden he wrapped his tiny fingers around my thumb.

Now, there are people who will say that it was just a reflex. But after that, 3:00 A.M. just didn't seem quite so bad anymore.

Marriage and the Modern Woman

As women gain greater recognition in society, their clearly defined submissive role in marriage has changed dramatically to a more assertive one. With this change, the homeostasis of the marital dyad has been threatened. Ultimately, however, the potential benefits for women as well as men seem to far outweigh the temporary stress.

During this transition, women often experience the dilemma of wanting both the advantages of the submissive role as well as those of the dominant role.

Particularly in the last decade, standards and norms of behavior for women have been in a perpetual state of redefinition. In the process of attempting to correct previous injustices and to establish a more equal place in society, the modern woman frequently finds herself thrust into uncharted territory and plagued by self-doubt.

Still, the institution of marriage now offers more options than ever before to the woman willing to accept the challenge.

God knows it's not easy.

When you're not yourself

One spring, when I was filling out our tax return, I accidentally signed it on the line marked "Your signature."

"Drat!" I said. My immediate reaction was that I'd have to fill out the whole page all over again.

It's a funny thing. When you get married, the words "your signature" suddenly don't mean your signature anymore. They mean your husband's signature most of the time, even if you filled out the form, which you most likely did.

After I thought about it for a while, it occurred to me that there was probably no legal reason why I couldn't sign on the "your signature" line and let Ralph sign on "spouse's signature." He was, after all, a spouse. Right?

Wrong.

"Hey," he said when he saw the return, "you signed in the wrong place."

"It said 'your signature.' That's my signature."

"But they didn't mean you. They meant me."

"Then they should have said so."

"Since when have you been 'you'?"

"As Tarzan would have said, 'Me, you; you, spouse.' If you want to be 'you,' you have to fill out the form."

"You don't have to be so literal about it."

"Well, what kind of schizophrenia-producing deal is it when they're always asking for 'your signature' and you write somebody else's name? No wonder women don't know who they are."

"I'm taking away your Emma Goldman book," said Ralph, signing on the "spouse's signature" line.

After that, there was no holding me back. Every form I filled out — for memberships, mailing lists, registrations — I gleefully filled in my name in the "your name" space, and under "spouse's name," I wrote "Ralph." It was almost frighteningly exhilarating.

Of course, a lot of places changed it back. I guess you have to expect that. Even though you know you're "you," they don't.

What really discouraged me, though, was when some of our mail started coming to *Mr.* Louise DeGrave.

Child care made hard

When I talked to friends about hiring a housekeeper to help take care of our baby while I worked, they all said how hard it was to find someone who didn't just sit in front of the tube all day and ignore the kid.

So we insisted on a very careful screening before we hired Vira.

Come back, housekeepers who just sit in front of the tube all day and ignore the kid. All is forgiven.

I don't really mean that, of course. Vira was wonderfully warm and maternal with Alan. She said she felt like Alan was her own son. In retrospect, however, that was part of the problem.

Now, I'll be the first to admit that a little assertiveness on my part at the beginning would have gone a long way. Alas, I didn't have the foggiest notion how to be an employer. Both Ralph and I grew up in families where if the house needed painting, you all went out and painted it. In my defense, however, I think Vira was secretly taking the Dale Carnegie course on weekends.

The upshot of all this was that somehow (I think I just explained how), Vira and I ended up in a custody battle over Alan.

I can't remember exactly how it started, but gradually I began to notice that Vira kept taking the baby into her room and closing the door. Now, while I was working, this was fine.

One afternoon, however, I was working at home and didn't seem to be progressing, so I decided to take a break and play with the baby. His little bassinet was empty so I knocked on Vira's door.

Vira stuck her head out. "What do you want?" she said.

"Well, um, I was hoping to see the baby," I said.

"I'm sorry, he's sleeping now," she told me firmly. "Try back in an hour."

"Oh, OK," I said, schlepping off into the woodwork.

Ralph couldn't see what the problem was when I first tried to explain it to him.

"So why did you let her get away with it?" he said. "Who's running the show around here, anyway?"

The following week, however, I had to go out to a meeting one night.

"Did you have a nice evening with the baby?" I asked Ralph when I returned.

"Actually, I didn't see much of him," Ralph admitted. "Vira said it was time for him to go to sleep. You know, you ought to talk to her about being so bossy."

The next night, however, we came home late and found the baby in bed. With Vira. That mobilized us to action. We told her that Alan was not to be in her room at any time under any circumstances. Period.

"You're just jealous," she pouted. (And you thought I was kidding about Dale Carnegie.)

"Precisely," said Ralph.

Well, anyway, that settled that. For the brief remaining time she was with us until I phased out of my job, she abided by the rule and never brought Alan into her room anymore. I learned the hard way that it really pays to be clear right in the beginning.

And contrary to my fears, we saw no signs of reprisal. She still let us play with him whenever we wanted to.

Booby traps

I've known for a long time that life isn't fair. But never have I felt it so acutely as the day when my exceedingly well-endowed friend, Esther, underwent a breast-reduction operation.

Only someone who has spent her teenage years sauntering into lingerie shops, flinging her long blond hair over her shoulder, and inquiring in an earthy voice, "What do you have in a black lace training bra?" can truly appreciate the anguish Esther's surgery caused me.

Actually, until Esther told me about it, I didn't even know such an operation existed. I still haven't decided whether it should be morally permissable while there are those of us going without.

Esther, of course, insists that the pectorally oriented general public has no concept of the physical pain that an excess of mammary tissue can produce. Frankly, however, it is hard to really empathize with someone whose lingerie is digging into her shoulders from the weight when yours, unless glued to your rib cage, wanders up around your neck.

I guess it was early in my adolescence when I first realized that in this world, there are the haves and the have-nots.

Mother used to try to console me about not being well endowed like my best friend, Bonnie, by telling me that it would be "down to her waist by the time she's forty." This, however, was no consolation to me when it was up to her eyeballs at fifteen.

I still remember the anguish of finally persuading my mother to take me to a department store for my first set of adult lingerie, and finding all the lacy garments of my selection to be too big.

"Have you something smaller than an A?" inquired Mother of the saleswoman.

"You mean, like an A-minus?" she said. I was so embarrassed, I just wanted to crawl into the nearest 38-D and hide. After considerable discussion and some formal measurement, it was determined that they did not carry my size (a 28-concave, I think) and that I should perhaps wait and come back next year.

The situation did improve, of course, as it is wont to do, but in retrospect, it was probably not the wisest choice for me to insist on wearing a strapless dress to my high-school junior prom. My best friend, Bonnie, kept repeating her mother's admonition not to bend over or "men" (my date came up to about my waistband) would look down the front. "If they do," I said finally in exasperation, "the only thing they will see is my feet!" Every time I exhaled, I had to hold the dress up manually.

Well, anyway, Esther had her surgery, and within a short time, she was fully recovered. As for me, it took several more weeks.

Women as their own worst enemies

I have often thought that women are their own worst enemies.

For the first six years of our marriage, it always seemed that Ralph and I went over to friends' homes for supper, and thirty seconds after we walked in the door, we womenfolk would retire to the kitchen to cook and set the table and trip over small children and pets, while the menfolk retired to the living room to slurp dip and wax cerebral.

After dinner, it was the same routine.

In someone else's home, I wouldn't have dreamed (except occasionally) of inflicting my views on other people. But in my own home, I gradually came to adhere to the maxim "I work, ergo men cook."

It was during a continuous stream of long-term houseguests that year that I tentatively tried out a new ruling that every houseguest over the age of eighteen, male or female, who stayed over three days was required to cook and do dishes on a rotating basis. Now here was the clincher: Wives were not permitted to substitute for husbands.

I was expecting some of the men to get temporarily bent out of shape about it all. Alas, it was my women friends who protested.

"Um, Louise," said my visiting friend, Cathy. "Jeremy doesn't know how to cook."

"Oh, it doesn't have to be fancy," I said. "Jeremy can make

TV dinners on his night. I'll show him how to turn on the oven."

"But you don't understand, Louise. I just couldn't let Jeremy cook or do dishes."

"Sure you can," I said soothingly. "Take a tranquilizer, go out for a long walk, and before you know it, it'll be over."

Meanwhile, my husband, Ralph, the sadist, was listening in with that obnoxious Cheshire grin he reserves for such occasions. He loves to watch me get nailed to the wall on this kind of issue. I might add, however, that he's an excellent cook, and adequate, if reluctant, dishwasher.

"But," said Cathy anxiously, "if I let Jeremy cook and clean up, what does he need *me* for?"

You had to say it, didn't you, Cathy. My head knows it's not true. But my heart still wonders.

Father just likes you to *think* he knows best

When we first got little Alan, I was really worried that Ralph might start taking his father's advice.

"Sure, kids are a lot of work," said Pop, leaning back comfortably in his chair. "But there are ways to get around it."

"Like what?" said Ralph.

"Let Louise do it," said Pop.

Fortunately, Ralph turned out to be a very involved father. From the beginning, he and Alan would go off on long sight-seeing expeditions together, on foot or bicycle, with Alan in a front carrier — instead of a backpack — so they could "talk." This child has been places I still haven't been.

Ralph took him on countless trips to the zoo and beach, football games, all the major local parks, and even for a tour of his office building. ("This is where Daddy goes to earn money to support your diaper habit," explained Ralph at the latter.) The fact that the baby slept through the majority of these scenic attractions did not daunt Ralph one bit.

In the early days, they would have their nightly talks with the baby perched on top of the filing cabinet so they could see eye to eye, but once Alan could sit up alone, they sat on the floor for their tête-à-têtes. (It actually looked more like a tête-à-knee.) They splashed around in the bath and explored the yard in search of new textures and smells.

One day I heard deep, long coos of pleasure emanating from the baby's room and went to investigate. Ralph had stripped him down to his diaper and was giving him a massage with baby oil. For Christmas, Ralph bought Alan a toy, a sunhat for their walks, and an FM tuner so he could listen to classical music in his crib.

As I said, Ralph fortunately did not follow in his father's footsteps. But a family legacy dies hard.

I remember when Alan was only about eight weeks old, and Ralph came back from taking him for a walk. The kid not only had a diaperful, but promptly proceeded to spit up all over himself.

"Want to clean him up?" I said as I mixed a batch of formula.

"Oh, no," said Ralph, attempting to hand the baby over. "It is the mundane acts of child care that help a mother form an intimate attachment with her infant. I think it's important that I not interfere."

There are times when a simple look expresses far more than words ever could. Ralph got one.

"Well," he shrugged as he headed off to the changing table, "it was worth a try."

"Ralph," I said, "your father would have been proud of you."

Actually, if there was one complaint I had about Ralph, it was that he was maybe a little *too* good with the baby. There were times when I wondered if I could continue to be compatible with a man who seemed to have infinite patience toward little children.

In my defense, I have to say that it is much easier to be a serene parent when you only see a child a few hours a day, as

Ralph did. This is especially true when the child is being a royal grouch.

I remember, for example, when little Alan got his first DPT shot. The poor nubbins cried for three solid days. Finally the pediatrician prescribed some phenobarbital for him, but probably more for me than for him.

Ralph, however, was horrified. *"Drug* our baby?" he gasped when he came home at 11:00 P.M. from watching the tennis tournament he'd gone to straight from work. "I can't *believe* you'd even *consider* such a thing."

Five minutes later, the baby, who had been crying nonstop since seven that morning, finally fell asleep, exhausted (without phenobarbital). "Besides," said Ralph, "I don't know why his crying bothers you so much. It doesn't bother *me."*

(Did I mention that this was as close as we ever got to divorce? And that it was *very* close?)

Of course, Ralph hadn't been Patience Personified 100 percent of the time either. He'd had his moments. One morning, after he'd done three night feedings, Ralph, the same man who thought phenobarbital constituted child abuse, suggested putting a nasogastric tube down the kid's stomach and hooking it up to a continuous milk supply.

But that had been five months before, and in the intervening time, I had hardly seen more than a slightly crazed look in Ralph's eye after a babysitting stint. In most ways, of course, I was delighted. Who could knock a perennially calm, patient, understanding father?

Unfortunately, I could. Just once, sadistic though this sounds, I was hoping that just as Ralph got Alan all ready for a pediatrician's appointment (for which they were already late), that the baby would suddenly throw up all over his clean outfit at the same time as the dog attacked the mailman, the phone rang, and two tenacious Mormons showed up at the door to discuss Ralph's spiritual future. Just once, I wanted to see Ralph get a little flustered too.

But it never happened.

One afternoon in February, however, I left the baby with Ralph while I did a long list of errands. When I walked in the door several hours later, there was Ralph engaged in seemingly rapturous play with Alan.

"How'd you make out?" I inquired.

"Oh, just great!" said Ralph, delineating a long string of ecstatic activities he'd enjoyed with the baby as he attempted to hand Alan over to me.

"Actually," I said, unloading a grocery bag, "would you watch him for another hour or so while I unpack this stuff and put something together for dinner?"

When I got no answer, I looked up. Not only had the broad smile disappeared from Ralph's face, but suddenly he looked more tired than I had ever seen him.

"I don't want you to think in any way that I didn't have fun," Ralph assured me earnestly. "But I was thinking it might be fun to try the new Peruvian place on the corner."

"But we can't take the baby there," I said.

Ralph's eyes lit up like a Christmas tree. "Precisely," he said.

How to be assertive without getting annihilated: A survivor's story

The one thing my assertiveness-training book didn't tell me was how come, whenever I tried being assertive in a new situation, I had this overwhelming feeling I was going to get annihilated?

I was very sensitive about being annihilated. This may have been why, for the first twenty-six years of my life, I had the assertiveness of a bowl of linguini.

One night, however, Ralph and I were at our favorite restaurant and there were these people at the next table who sounded as if they'd been taking shouting lessons for years. I mean, they couldn't even say "pass the salt" in less than ninety decibels.

Prolonged loud noise really makes me tense and nervous.

Even Ralph, who never even noticed that our Colorado house was almost under the airport flight path, was beginning to show signs of stress. We were not enjoying our meal at all.

"I wish someone would tell those people to shut up!" I said finally.

Ralph's eyes lit up immediately.

"You know," he said, "you've been getting really good at things like that."

OK, I'll admit that I'd done some pretty assertive things lately. But I had never told anyone at a restaurant to be quiet. You didn't *do* things like that. You put up with it, had a rotten time, then went home and wrote Ann Landers asking her to please tell people to be more considerate. That's what you did.

"You want me to tell six *men* to be quiet?" I said incredulously.

It was an absurd idea. Until the people at the next table got even louder.

"Um, ah . . . I don't know quite how to say this, but I, um, was wondering if maybe you could talk a little more quietly. I mean, not a lot, just a little."

As soon as I said it, I wished I hadn't. I was going to get killed. For sure. Why did I *do* things like this?

"Oh, of course, honey. We're really sorry."

I realized that they were just pretending to take me seriously. Any second they were going to make a cruel joke at my expense.

". . . We had no idea we were being so noisy. Guess we just got carried away with our conversation."

I always knew masochism paid. If I got out of this alive, I was never going to be assertive again.

". . . You see, we just found out that three of us went to the same high school."

Looked like they were going to string me along like this, then humiliate me horribly somehow. In public yet. I wanna go home.

". . . So please let us know if we get too noisy again."

"Excuse me?" I said.

"Let us know if we get too noisy again."

"You're incredible," said Ralph as I sat down again. "I don't know what you said, but they're suddenly much quieter."

"I'm alive," I said dazedly. "Not even an obscene gesture." I still can't quite believe it when it works.

In-laws: The second visit

Friday: Ralph's parents arrived today from Florida to see Alan for the first time. Despite Ralph's careful routing (this was only the folks' third flight ever), Mom and Pop (and the dog) missed their connection when they were called off the plane minutes before take-off for an "emergency" phone call from Cousin Ethel's nursing home. Cousin Ethel, who is ninety-four, was apparently a spry lady until a stroke two years ago; since then she hasn't recognized anyone. Since Mom and Pop live near the nursing home, they manage Ethel's affairs. Nursing home told them that Ethel had been taken to the hospital due to internal bleeding but was "OK."

Due to missed connection, folks and dog were forced to change both planes and airlines in Dallas and Los Angeles. Ralph heard that and gave up hope of ever seeing them again. All arrived eventually, however, the worse for wear.

Our small house is loaded to the rafters: Ralph, me, baby, housekeeper, Mom, Pop, three dogs (ours, vacationing friend's, and dog-in-law). Dogs not hitting it off well. Three male dogs perhaps two too many.

Saturday: Ralph and housekeeper succumbed to terrible malady last night, later diagnosed as salmonella poisoning secondary to leftover chicken salad. Ralph spent day wishing self dead. Wished housekeeper dead too. Busy day with trips to pharmacy for Compazine, ministrations to sick.

Hospital in Florida called. Ethel took turn for worse. Underwent surgery but not stable. Folks quite distressed.

Dogs not getting along at all. Keep one in back, one in front, one in house, rotate at intervals.

Sunday: Medical bulletin: Ralph better; housekeeper not, so sent home; Ethel failing. Alfred (our dog) suffering massive regression in form of relieving self on living-room furniture.

Read in paper that Motel-on-the-Mountain where Ralph and I spent wedding night is now a homosexual resort. Is nothing sacred?

Monday: Mom biopsied for skin cancer. Ethel critical. Ralph's father opened door for UPS man, who was assaulted by phalanx of ferocious dogs. Dogs not man-eating but who could tell? Neither UPS man nor postman (assaulted Saturday) speaking to us.

Letter from firm in Illinois to check serial numbers on our smoke detectors as they may be fire hazards.

Tuesday: Housekeeper (Vira) returned. Have been feeling nervous. House very noisy: dishwasher, vacuum, clothes washer, radio, phone, dogfights, baby crying, TV on extra loud because Mom hard of hearing.

Hospital in Florida called midafternoon that Ethel had succumbed. Helped Pop make funeral arrangements. Many logistical problems: body in Florida, funeral in New York, Mom and Pop here.

Wednesday: Spent all morning at dentist. Came home with pain radiating into ear. Took two Tylenol with codeine and spent afternoon in coma.

Thursday: Put baby down for morning nap, turned around to see our car (parked on the street) hit and run. Fortunately license number of offenders taken by nice lawyer driving by. Hour later, two teenagers showed up at house professing to have seen error of their ways. Had also seen me talking to police and witness. Kids had only had car two days. No license, no registration, no permit, no insurance. Asked them if they'd considered fleeing across border. Difficulty negotiating partly due to dogfight in living room. Eventually we, they, police, insurance company came to agreement.

Mom's biopsies negative. All much relieved.

Friday: Took Mom and Pop to airport for flight to funeral.

Dog jumped on Ralph's lap while Ralph driving on freeway. Ralph barely missed Safeway truck.

At gate, kissed folks good-bye. Mom said, "Thank God everything went smoothly."

The wife as mobile rescue squad

I think many women will identify with me when I say that some husbands have a tendency to take advantage of our good natures.

It's a problem, it really is. You love the guy and you get pleasure from taking care of him. Not in a masochistic or servile way, but out of mutual caring and respect. And when he calls and needs a special favor, you want to help him out.

But why does the poor schlemiel have to need a special favor every day?

Take my husband, Ralph, for example. A terrific guy and all, it's just that he has this tendency not to notice the little things in life, like that his gas gauge is three notches below empty.

He wonders if you would mind retrieving the raincoat he thinks he left at last night's restaurant, deliver his forgotten briefcase to the office, and, though he hates to impose on you, could you go down to Motor Vehicles and get a duplicate of his lost auto registration that he forgot he got a ticket for because he has just received a warrant for his arrest?

I wouldn't want to say that Ralph is absentminded. I would prefer to say that he suffers from a terminal case of selective inattention.

For a while, this was getting to be a serious problem in our marriage. After spending several weeks analyzing a recurrent dream that I was a doormat, I knew I simply had to stop rescuing Ralph when he screwed up.

Several afternoons later, I was just leaving my office for lunch when the phone rang. "It's for you, Louise," said a coworker. "It's Ralph."

I picked up the phone. "The answer is no," I said.

"What do you mean, no," said Ralph. "I haven't said anything yet."

"It's still no," I said.

"My car just stopped on Torrey Pines Road," said Ralph.

"Too bad!" (This was so painful.)

"I might be out of gas or it might be something mechanical."

An ambiguous situation. I wavered. (Never waver.)

"And I was wondering, since you're only five blocks away . . ."

"That's irrelevant to the issue," I said.

"And I have two clients waiting for me in my office, one of whom came all the way from Los Angeles with her retarded child . . ."

Well, it just wasn't fair to punish Ralph's clients. Not to mention that his new business was still rather tenuous and he could ill afford to alienate people. And it could be a mechanical problem beyond Ralph's control.

So off I went with the gas can, picked up Ralph from his phone booth, and he drove us back to his car. With a gallon of gas, it started right up.

"Ralph," I said, "I'm very relieved that it's not a mechanical problem. But as for your running out of gas, there's something I'd like to say to you as soon as I can think of something sadistic enough."

"I'm really sorry, Louise," said Ralph. He was really sorry.

I shook my head resignedly as I waved good-bye to Ralph and went back to my car. I had to admit it was very hard to stay angry at Ralph very long. He was just so kind and loving. As I got in my car, I reflected on the enormous pressures he was under in his business. Small wonder he forgot things occasionally.

It was then that I realized that he had just driven off with my car keys.

"Will someone be home all day Friday?"

I think if there is one phrase that really sums up the oppression of women, it is "Will someone be home all day Friday?"

Now, I will allow that there are a certain number of women who do spend a majority of their time at home. At various times I have even been one of them.

But even if I did nothing but watch soap operas all day, I would have to get out to the supermarket eventually. After all, woman does not live by *The Edge of Night* alone.

For reasons I could never fathom, it is beyond the cognitive capabilities of a large segment of the working world to consider the possibility that a woman's time might have any value. The worst offenders, I think, are construction workers, repair persons, and delivery persons.

One should understand that when, for example, a repair service asks if you will be home Friday, they are not so much inquiring about your plans as making a statement about them. What they're really saying behind the ostensible effort to accommodate your schedule is, "You want your washer fixed, lady, somebody better be home Friday!"

Now, you hadn't planned to be home Friday, but they've got you over a barrel (or a lint filter, anyway), so even if you work outside the home, you find yourself telling the man that yes, you'll be home Friday.

By some process of deduction I've never been able to figure out, repair services interpret your willingness to be home Friday as an assumption that you had planned to be home Friday *anyway*. And rushing headlong down the path of illogic, it stands to reason that a woman who usually spends Fridays at home is probably at home Mondays through Thursdays too.

Ergo, it is not necessary to show up on Friday.

It is also not necessary to let you know they're not coming Friday, because they're not really inconveniencing you since it was their understanding you were going to be home Friday *anyway*. Didn't they ask you specifically if you were going to be there?

(I'll bet the guy who first described the Double-Bind Theory actually got it from his wife, who was home waiting for the Roto-Rooter man.)

So about 4:30 P.M. Friday, still repairless, you call them back (keeping a weary eye on your cranky housebound toddler who has long tired of his toys and is flushing your electric curlers down the toilet) and they say they are terribly sorry they won't be able to come today after all. But will someone be home Monday?

It was after just such an experience that I came to the conclusion that unless I wanted to do this for the rest of my life, I was simply going to have to reorganize my life to make myself more independent of the need for repairs, deliveries, estimates, or what have you. I even developed a plan of action for this, worked out in some detail.

The only problem is, I'm just not sure I'd *like* living in a tent. . . .

Fleeting moments

Wanted: Eight-month-old baby and his mommy seeking time warp. Immediate reply requested as baby growing up (too) fast.

Having never been around babies much before, it continued to impress me what wonderful people they were. At eight months, Alan was at such a nice age that 95 percent of the time, I wished I really could have frozen us both in time. (Actually, I'd originally thought of time-warping only Alan instead of both of us, but then it occurred to me that it might not be so easy to dig him out from under the sofa when he was still eight months and I was eighty-six.)

It was at eight months that I really began mourning the loss of Alan's tiny-babyhood — all those times when I rocked him back and forth in the rocker with his little warm, peach-fuzz head nestled against my cheek, his tiny fist wrapped around my thumb. These days, when I picked him up to cuddle him, he still nestled his head next to my cheek—but only to get a better angle at the plant behind my head.

Here we'd waited years for him, and his babyhood was over so fast. When he grew out of the little green outfit he came home from the adoption agency in, I felt like crying. When he couldn't wear the little pin-striped sailor suit anymore, I actually did.

This was not to say that some of the loss of that cuddly baby of yestermonth wasn't compensated for by his dazzling array of new tricks. Some of the dazzle I could have done without, of course. ("No, no, Alan. Grape juice is not for heaving over the side of your high chair.") But where I once couldn't wait for him to take a nap so I could have a little time to myself, suddenly I found myself entranced, often for hours at a time, watching him play, discover, examine, and explore.

I guess I wanted it all—the intimacy of the tiny infant and the expanded repertoire of the older one. And I knew I couldn't have it.

One night, however, I was in the kitchen making dinner while Alan was off relentlessly pursuing an intensive, after-noon-long study of the dining room, an activity for which he had eschewed even his usual nap. Finally, of course, he simply ran out of steam, and try though he might, he just couldn't muster the energy to turn another stereo knob or peel back another bit of wallpaper from the wall. It was time to head homeward.

When I looked up a few minutes later, there was the pint-sized Lone Ranger plodding wearily toward his mommy across the great tundra of the kitchen floor, barely able to put one little hand in front of the other. Blinded by tears of fatigue, he promptly crashed into the refrigerator and col-lapsed into loud wails at my feet.

As soon as I picked him up, he stopped crying. Then he nestled his head against my cheek, wrapped his fist around my thumb, and went to sleep.

A half hour later when Ralph came home, I was still sitting in the rocker slowly rocking him back and forth.

"I think he's asleep," said Ralph. "Do you want me to put him in his crib?"

I just kept rocking. "No," I said softly, "not yet."

Coping with the male domestic disaster

I love Ralph, I really do. But I can't help but ask myself: Is it really possible that a man who graduated from college summa cum laude, Phi Beta Kappa, and with a physics prize is still, after ten years, incapable of mastering the operation of a washing machine which entails turning a knob to "on" and pushing a button marked "start"? Is it even conceivable that this same man cannot go to a supermarket and return with all nine items on a list and both shoes of the child who accompanied him, wash a pot such that there is not mold growing in it six days later, or load a dishwasher in such a way that nothing is broken/mangled/melted?

It's not that I don't appreciate Ralph's willingness to help me with the domestic chores, because I really do. But when he does help, is it too much to ask that he (a) finish a job he starts, (b) meet the health standards of a tenement and, (c) execute the job in such a way that the final results don't take an hour of *my* time to rectify?

Take the dishes, for example. Now, Ralph is very good about offering to do the dishes. Unfortunately, he considers "doing the dishes" just that: washing two plates, two glasses, and two forks. He has this tendency to overlook certain other details of the job that need attending to. These include cleaning the pots and pans, table top, counters, and stove.

I think what really began tó bother me about the dishes was

that while Ralph was getting all the credit for washing them, I was actually doing most of the work. Something seemed to be vaguely inequitable about this arrangement.

At first I simply tried pointing out in a nice way some of the deficiencies of the job. ("Um, Ralph, you did a nice job on the dishes as far as you went, but I'm wondering if you'd be willing to finish the other eighty percent?") But Ralph just got in a huff and said I was being "critical."

Then someone suggested to me that I might try simply praising him for the parts he did well, leaving out altogether the things he didn't do, in hopes that the praise would motivate him to do better. But it didn't, and besides, it never came out sounding quite right. ("Hey, Ralph, you did a *super* job putting those two unrinsed plates in the dishwasher, and I really want to thank you.") Ralph sensed my lack of sincerity and said I was "ungrateful."

When neither of these worked, I decided I would simply accept it. Ralph, after all, had many endearing qualities, even if he was terrible at housework. So rather than fight about it, I would genuinely, from the bottom of my heart, thank him for waxing the kitchen floor, even if he hadn't swept it or washed it first. The only problem with this solution was I could never figure out what to do with the intense violent impulses I felt toward Ralph afterward.

Finally, not long ago, I decided that all along, I had been taking the wrong tack. Here, after all, was a highly intelligent man. I would *reason* with him.

"Ralph," I said carefully one morning, "let's say I was your secretary and you needed ten letters typed. Let's say I did the first two well, but the next three were so full of misspellings as to be unsendable. On top of that, I accidentally erased the other five letters from the tape so that you had to redictate them. Tell me honestly, Ralph. Would you thank me?"

"Of course not," said Ralph. "I'd fire you."

"So?" I said triumphantly.

"So what?" said Ralph.

"So, do you get the analogy?" I said.

"What analogy?" said Ralph.

"Well," I said, "that it's hard for me to thank *you* when you do a lousy job on the dishes."

"But," said Ralph, looking perplexed, "the dishes aren't *important*."

I have this awful feeling I might be thirty years too late.

Guilt

When my father asked my sister, Marie, what she'd like as a first-baby gift, Marie replied, "Louise." So Dad sent me a plane ticket so that I could go help Marie after the baby was born.

I, of course, was delighted. Marie and I are only a year apart in age, and with the exception of a few years during high school, we have always been very close. (In high school, she was the "smart" one and I was the "popular" one. As soon as she started having dates and I started having an IQ, we got along much better.)

I would be less than honest, however, if I said that Ralph's initial reaction to my proposed absence was one of unqualified enthusiasm. When it gets right down to it, I think what rankled Ralph most was not that I was planning to leave him two weeks with the baby, but where I was going that he wasn't. Er, did I mention that my sister lives in England?

Actually, I could well understand Ralph's feelings. If given a choice between two weeks in the English countryside or staying home and going to work, the average person would not think long. However, as I pointed out to Ralph, he did not have a very pregnant sister in England and I did. (He has a brother in New Jersey, but who ever said life was fair?)

The major bugaboo about this trip, of course, was little Alan. I really didn't want to leave him for such a long time, but who, I asked myself, would willingly and with forethought take a sixteen-month-old dynamo on a twenty-two-hour trip to a nonbabyproofed house and an eight-hour time difference? And since I was supposed to be devoting my energies to helping Marie, he would probably be far happier at home with his dad, his teddy bear, and his favorite sitter.

Ralph couldn't have agreed more, but in the weeks before the trip, little jokes began to emerge about how I shouldn't worry about Alan because I was leaving him for valid reasons, but that we should probably start saving for his psychoanalysis (and none of that short-term, three-or-four-year stuff either). Not that I needed Ralph to instill any more guilt in me; I had enough of my own. (During a severe attack of it one night, I finally blurted out miserably, "What if I promise not to have a good time?")

Even worse, alas, than the thought of little Alan pining away for me was the thought that he wouldn't. I kept having this recurring fantasy of returning home and having Alan point to me and inquire dispassionately of his non-English-speaking sitter, "Quien es esta mujer?"

In an attempt to assuage my guilty feelings, I stocked the refrigerator and freezer before I left with two weeks' worth of everybody's favorite foods, arranged round-the-clock help for Ralph, bought a nice present for everyone, and left endearing notes all over the house scientifically calculated to be found when my credit might be lowest.

None of this, however, made my leave-taking any less painful. A moment I never wish to repeat is standing there at the gate at the airport looking desperately back and forth between the tearful sixteen-month-old baby clinging to one hand and the ticket to London clutched in the other. I think this is what's known as a conflict.

But then I was finally on the plane and soaring out over the ocean. And gradually I stopped crying and began to fondle my shiny new passport and played with my English money and looked at the pictures on the postcards Marie had sent. And all of a sudden, this almost overwhelming feeling came over me. *WHOOPEE!*

The family worrier

Every family needs a family worrier — a person who worries about everything from world peace to whether there will be two seats together at the movie theater. Someone, after all, has to worry about whether the local mom-and-pop grocery will stay in business, the house will get robbed, or the baby will get sick the day before you leave on vacation.

The reason, of course, that I think every family needs a family worrier is that I have always been the worrier in my family.

Being a family worrier is an extremely demanding job. Not only do you have to worry about the likely things that can go wrong, but the unlikely things as well. This requires tremendous imaginative capabilities.

To be a successful family worrier, one must subscribe to two fundamental principles. The first and most crucial is that no matter what anybody else tells you, nature abhors a confident person. That is to say, let one disastrous possibility go unworried about and you can just about guarantee it will happen to you.

The second basic law of worrydom is that there is a first time for everything. Just because Ralph has never broken both legs skiing doesn't mean it can't happen. To be on the safe side, it is always better to worry about it.

Just before a trip, I worry even more than usual, even though Ralph and I rarely have catastrophes while traveling. This is because I have long subscribed to the "worry now, enjoy later" plan. Once everything that can go wrong has been worried about, I can just relax and enjoy the trip.

From time to time, Ralph has tried to convince me that it is not the worrying itself that ensures a pleasant trip but my thorough planning and preparation. But then, what does Ralph know?

The problem with being a family worrier is that it is a thankless job. There you are worrying your heart out for people, and are they the least bit grateful?

We were on a plane a while back and coincidentally met our good friend Susan, who hates flying and was convinced that if she relaxed for even a moment, the plane would crash. Now, I really like flying and don't usually engage in more than a few token minutes' anxiety about it. But as I told Susan, it was a good feeling to know that someone was in there worrying —just in case.

I guess the part that really rankles me most about being the family worrier, though, is that after all my hard work, I end up looking tense and uptight and Ralph comes off looking like Mr. Casual.

"Ralph," I said, "I'd like for you to start doing some of the worrying for a change."

"But I'm not worried," said Ralph.

"That's exactly my point. Of course, I'll still take charge of the global worrying and the prevention of major disasters," I said. I wasn't sure I'd trust Ralph to worry enough to keep the postearthquake tidal wave from hitting our house anyway. "But I do think you could start taking over some of the routine worries, like whether we have enough diapers to get home, the gas station will be open, the airport will be fogged in, there is salt in the picnic basket, the eight o'clock show at the movies will be sold out, or the mayonnaise in the refrigerator is still good."

"I'm sure things will turn out all right," said Ralph. "You just have to have a positive attitude."

I ask you, what can you do with a person like that?

Sitter power

I used to think I knew who the real power people were in this country, but I was wrong. The *real* power people are not bankers. They are not corporate executives or White House aides.

They are babysitters.

It wasn't until I became a mother that I learned that happiness is an obese adolescent neighbor with a lousy social life. I don't have one, but if we ever move again, you can bet I'll screen the neighborhood more carefully.

Almost every mother I talk to agrees that the sitter dilemma is the real bugaboo of motherhood. Some days you just can't find a competent sitter. Some days you can't even find an *in*competent sitter. So exasperating is the problem that parents can be driven to desperate lengths.

It is really awesome to contemplate as you drive to a dinner engagement on a Saturday night that you have just left your only child and the entire contents of your house in the hands of a fourteen-year-old stranger whose major qualification for the job was that she was available to come that night.

Actually, it has been my experience that daytime sitting is hardest to find. Fortunately, however, I have located a wonderful day-care mother with a heart of gold and nerves of steel who takes care of Alan (and four other children) during the hours I work. (Legend has it that this woman once took five toddlers into J. C. Penny's. There are those who think she should be awarded the Purple Heart for this.)

I think it would be safe to say that I am even more interested in this woman's health than she is. I'll bet if a scientist lined up twenty-five mothers and whispered the words "sick babysitter" in their ears, he'd get a statistically significant rise in pulse.

Finding nighttime sitters is a little less pressure because it's only your mental health rather than your employment that's involved. Every mother, of course, hoards in the depths of her address book her classified list of evening babysitters. I have often thought that the ultimate gift of love in this society is to divulge the phone number of one's best sitter to a friend in need. The ultimate act of ingratitude is if she passes it on.

I think what is most disconcerting of all about working with babysitters, though, is that the people you depend on so heavily take the job so casually. Teenagers are notorious in this regard. Nothing feeds one's general anxiety more than to accidentally run into one's sitter at the supermarket at 4:00 P.M. only to have her exclaim, "Hey, was I supposed to sit for you tonight?"

I was saying to a friend not long ago that in ten years life will seem so easy, not having to get a sitter. And she said, "No, in ten years you'll have a teenager instead." There are some situations in life where you don't ever win.

Ansel Adams never had it like this

When Alan was eighteen months old, I decided it would not be unreasonable to start taking some photography classes again. So I signed up for one at the university.

Photography, I discovered, is an altogether different proposition for a mother. It isn't that it can't be done and, indeed, enjoyed; it just takes a few more steps than it used to. Take the process of developing a roll of film, for example:

1. Put baby to bed. Kiss goodnight.
2. Find film-changing bag in toy box. Shake out cracker crumbs.
3. Stick arms in light-tight film bag, remove film from casing, load onto reels, and insert into developing tank.
4. Slice carrots over roast.
5. Pour developer into tank and begin timing for exactly seven minutes. Once per minute, agitate tank gently four to five times.
6. Transfer half the laundry from washer to dryer. Agitate tank.

7. Transfer other half laundry from washer to dryer. Agitate tank.

8. Let dog out. Agitate tank.

9. Rinse diaper pail. Agitate tank.

10. Get tap water to sixty-eight degrees. Wipe off high chair. Agitate tank while letting dog in. Get fixer ready.

11. Pour developer down drain. Rinse film thoroughly in running water. Start green beans.

12. Add fixer and begin timing for four minutes, agitating tank five seconds out of every thirty. Set table.

13. Rinse film in water. Stir green beans. Add hypoclearing agent. Agitate moderately for one to two minutes.

14. Wash film in running water for five minutes. Check on baby. Put chemicals away. Dress salad.

15. Fill tank with distilled water, add antiwetting agent, swish around. Greet husband. Remove film from reels and hang on drying clips.

16. Dip sponge in antiwetting solution, wipe film to prevent water marks.

17. Light candles.

18. Serve up.

The wife as nonperson

Shortly before we got Alan, I wrote a letter to our insurance company and signed it Louise DeGrave.

The reply came back addressed to Ralph. "Dear Mr. De-Grave," it began. "Thank you for your recent letter."

This was the (tragic) story of my married life. I corresponded with banks and insurance companies, and they corresponded with Ralph.

"How come nobody ever writes to *me*?" I lamented to Ralph, showing him the letter. "I mean, it's like I became incompetent on our wedding day."

"I guess there is a subtle message there," admitted Ralph.

"What's so subtle?" I said.

The irony of it all was, of course, that Ralph himself had written only two letters in our married life, and those only under duress. I even used to write to his mother for him. (She always replied, "Dear Ralph, Thank you for your recent letter" too, but I think that wasn't so much sexism as loathing.)

It didn't just happen with letters either; it happened on the phone too. Just a few weeks before, for example, Ralph and I had been thinking that in anticipation of being parents, we should maybe join a religious congregation. So I called up and talked to the guy in charge of membership, then I filled out the forms and mailed them in with a check.

About a week later, I answer the phone and a voice says, "Mrs. DeGrave? May I speak to your husband please?"

Well, I put Ralph on and it turns out to be the guy in charge of membership, who wants to clarify an item on the application that I had filled out and signed. When I realize who it is and what he wants, I decide I have an item of my own I'd like to clarify.

"Ralph," I said, "ask that turkey why he didn't just ask *me* that question when I answered the phone."

So Ralph says, very nicely, "Louise is wondering why you didn't ask her."

"Who's Louise?" he says.

"My wife," he says. "She answered the phone."

"Oh, *Mrs.* DeGrave," he says. "Oh, you see, I've been trying to get you at your office all week, but I wasn't able to reach you, so I just called the house. I usually try not to bother people at home on the weekends."

"I think she's wondering why you didn't call the house before," said Ralph.

"I didn't think you'd be there during the day," he says.

"I'm not explaining this very well," said Ralph. "I think Louise wants to know why you didn't call *her* at home."

"Why would I want to do that?" he said, genuinely confused.

"You know, women's lib," said Ralph. "I think she just wants you to know that she could have answered the question as well as I could. Probably better, actually, since she filled out the forms."

"Oh, women's *lib*," he says, it all becoming clearer. "Please assure Mrs. DeGrave that I have nothing against women. I just *always* deal with the man."

More guilt

After Alan's second birthday, I began reading various parenting manuals, not with the idea of following any particular one religiously, but more to get ideas on how I might handle such traditional toddler issues as toilet training and tantrums. And to be honest, I did get a lot of helpful advice.

But I also have to say, some of these child-care experts really know how to stick it to mothers.

As one reads along, one cannot help but notice a rather disconcerting tendency to suggest that if a kid turns out well, it's because he had good parents (plural). If, however, he is weird and funny-looking and talks to inanimate objects, everybody starts analyzing his relationship with his mother. (Face it. Have you ever even heard of a schizophrenogenic *father?*)

As I read along, I found myself suffering frequent palpitations over phrases like "the ultimate fulfillment of child rearing" (undoubtedly created by a eunuch who had never come in contact with a two-year-old) and "maternal instinct" (written by the same author to avoid a 2:00 A.M. feeding).

Anxiously I made lists of essential educational toys and experiences that the books insisted my child had to have, and worried endlessly that I'd already missed the critical period for promoting the proper hand-eye coordination that would ward off dyslexia.

I even worried that my child's toilet training had gone too smoothly and without the moderate degree of battle that some psychoanalysts feel is necessary to a child's developing autonomy. So even when things are going well, you have to worry that they aren't.

Child-care experts who don't write books also seemed to be skilled at making Mommy feel guilty. Calling nursery schools one afternoon, I encountered pronouncements like, "Our program is for children three and up. *(Pause.)* We don't believe children should be separated from their mothers before then." Or, "Our sessions are for two hours — about as long as a child this age should be away from his mother."

What gross psychological harm had I inflicted on my child, who had spent ten to twenty hours per week in day care since he was eleven months old? If I returned after two hours, he'd probably wonder what I was doing back so soon.

I think, though, that the kiddie-manual phrase that really did me in was, "In stressful situations, try to remain calm. Remember, your child is looking to you to be a role model in handling his own feelings."

A fine principle and one I strive to live up to, but have these people never been around the average household at 5:00 P.M.? Have they ever tried to put together a meal with a cranky toddler who is testing every limit he ever knew, who clings to your leg like a dragging anchor as you move back and forth from counter to stove, and who turns up the volume on the TV set to 130 decibels just as you're trying to fend off a tenacious vacuum-cleaner salesman and a solicitation for the Olympic volleyball team?

Fourteen times you patiently but firmly remove him from an offending activity with a quick scolding and offer an acceptable toy in replacement. But he is undeterred. The fifteenth time, you throw down your spatula, grab the kid, and bellow, "DO THAT ONE MORE TIME AND MOMMY WILL BREAK YOUR LITTLE NECK!" Just then you notice your husband standing in the door.

"Louise!" he says, shocked. "I thought we agreed we would *never* threaten our child with violence."

Feeling like the rottenest, most foul-tempered mommy in the world (to say nothing of your inadequacies as a human being), you slither back to the kitchen and weep silently into the casserole.

Frailty, thy name may not be woman. But guilt, thy name *is* mother.

To dream the impossible dream

Every mother has a secret dream for her child. Mine is that he grow up knowing how to hang up a shirt. Even if I couldn't get through to Ralph about his sloppy habits, I told myself, at least I didn't have to perpetuate his legacy of sloth for another generation. Which is why it was extremely disconcerting to realize that Ralph was quietly, ever-so-subtly undermining my efforts.

Don't get me wrong. Ralph has many wonderful qualities. He's responsible, bright, has a good business sense, a compassionate heart, and more musical, artistic, and athletic talents than any one person should be allowed to have. I will be delighted if Alan acquires some of these attributes.

I mean, it wasn't as though I was standing over Alan with a whip terrorizing him into picking up his Tinker Toys. But from the time he was eighteen months old, I have asked him to help me put away his playthings before bed. He didn't have to do much; usually he "helped" me by putting the Legos in the block bin and the blocks in the Lego bin. (Funny thing, that's exactly what his father does too. I may have just isolated Ralph's stage of developmental arrest.) God knows I could have done it myself in half the time. It was the *concept*.

Now, the one problem with being married to a slob is that the spouse automatically gets labeled a compulsively neat housekeeper. In our case, nothing could be farther from the truth. I vacuum once every three weeks, whether it needs it or not. In ten years, I have never stripped a kitchen floor. (Fortunately, yellow is my favorite color.) I have even considered running for office on an anti-ironing platform.

While we're on the subject, I have always regarded ironing as one of life's great useless activities. Left up to me, it would be declared a misdemeanor. After all, what do you have at the end of it except the prospect that the same garment is going to be staring you in the face again next week?

In comparison, Sisyphus got off easy, just having to push that rock up the hill. If they'd *really* wanted to stick it to him, they could have condemned him to eternal life as a housewife with a large family, pre–permanent press.

With the exception of Ralph's suits and shirts, buying an ironable has been strictly prohibited in my household for some years. Violating garments are sentenced to a minimum of six months in the ironing pile, followed by eventual parole to the Salvation Army box.

So I'd hardly call myself a fanatic housekeeper. Indeed, the only reason it's such an issue is that I hate housework so much that I am driven not to mess up the house in the first place.

In my further defense, I would like to say that it honestly doesn't bother me if Ralph wants to bring out every single one of Alan's toys when they play together. I think it's great that Ralph and Alan have such a close relationship. I just wish that at some point, eventually, within the next three to four weeks, they would put it all away again.

Ralph, however, gets completely bent out of shape when I bring up these petty details.

"I only had a half hour before going to the office," he insists defensively, "and I wanted it to be high-quality time. I *refuse* to waste my very limited playtime with my son harassing myself with your neurotic rules about cleanup."

"So what makes you think *I* want to harass myself cleaning it up either?" I said. (They say men marry their mothers. In our case, this was not true. When Ralph married me, I was nothing like his mother. He's just been trying to turn me into her ever since.)

"Well, I thought that under the circumstances, you'd be—"

"Happy you were entertaining Alan."

"Well, that's right, and that—"

"Just this once . . ."

"Well, just this once, because of—"

"My considerable gratitude . . ."

"Well, you know, I do work pretty darn hard to support you. That you'd be—"

"Glad to pick up all those toys."

"Well, yes."

"No."

As I explained to Ralph, picking up toys with Alan could be quality time too. You could make a game out of it. But more importantly, I explained, waxing eloquent, we would be teaching our son to be a responsible, considerate person, one who will respect the rights of others, who will understand the true meaning of cooperation, who will never expect or desire servitude from others.

So what does Ralph do after this impassioned speech? He corrals Alan in his room where I overhear him say, "We have to clean this up or Mommy will get mad."

I stormed in there. "WE ARE NOT CLEANING THIS UP FOR MOMMY OR SO THAT MOMMY WILL NOT GET MAD. IS THAT PERFECTLY CLEAR?"

"Oh, OK," said Ralph. "Alan, we are not cleaning this up for Mommy, or so that Mommy will not get mad." (Poor deluded Mommy.) "We are putting away the toys so that the house will look, um, *nice.*"

To give Ralph credit, he has improved some since that day. Both he and Alan are getting better at putting things away. It's not that Ralph agrees with me on a philosophical level. After all, he points out, he never cleaned up anything in his life and look at what a nice person *he* is. But because he loves me and because this issue is so obviously important to me, in the name of parental consistency, and as a special "gift" to me, he is willing to enforce the rule about Alan picking up his toys.

Five years ago, I never would have settled for this, insisting instead on philosophical as well as behavioral change. Now, however, I'll take what I can get.

Whether this shows growth or defeat, I'm still trying to decide.

Beauty, masochism, Satan, and contact lenses

For many millennia, the Devil contemplated how to make the vain (particularly women) suffer hell on earth, and in desperation, he finally consulted with a team of French designers who were all Down There serving long terms and were specialists at this sort of thing.

The French designers met together and came up with such diabolical items as bustles and corsets and long-line panty girdles, and cruelest of all, spike-heeled and platform shoes. Devil introduced them on earth, saying, "This shall fix the vain but good." But lo, it all went out of style.

This made the Devil quite irritated and so, knowing that if you want something done right you have to do it yourself, he went back to the drawing board and an idea more diabolical than ever emerged. Chortling delightedly to himself, the Devil proclaimed, "They shall wear contact lenses."

And so demonically successful was his idea that every year at the annual Devil's Workshop, a film about it is still shown, the first sequence of which focuses on women sitting in ophthalmologists' offices the world over mangling their eyeballs as they (vainly) attempt to learn how to get the contact lenses in and out before being sent home with a wearing schedule, a sterilizer, and a truckload of Boil 'n' Soak.

The second sequence of the film focuses in on a young wearer of the hard contact lenses. A voice-over explains that while the hard contacts relieve the vain of less of their cash, they are doomed to walk around squinty and bug-eyed, feeling like they have rocks in their eyes, which they do, and destined to spend half their lives crawling around on all fours pawing the grass looking for a microscopic lens, which has this remarkably annoying habit of popping out at the most inconvenient times. The voice-over remarks that these same individuals wouldn't dream of trying to find a needle in a haystack, but think nothing of looking for a contact lens in the south pasture.

The middle sequence of the film shows the same hard-contact-lens wearer getting absolutely fed up one day and flushing her two-hundred-dollar lenses down the nearest toilet, which, of course, is exactly what the Devil and the American Optometric Association had in mind in the first place.

And the next sequence shows this same individual being relieved of a large amount of cash but not minding too much because she's heard that the soft lenses (although requiring an advanced degree in sterile technique) are much more comfortable and don't tend to fall out on the grass so much, which is true. So instead of crawling around on the grass, the soft-contact-lens wearer is shown going *"Arrrrrrgggggghhhhh"* with discomfort after she puts the lenses in inside out by mistake and subsequently going to pieces when she gets the right and left lenses mixed up and puts each in the wrong eye, leaving her legally blind and psychotic.

And in the final sequence of the film, a young San Diego mother and contact-lens wearer is interviewed and they ask her why the devil (you should excuse the expression) she wears contact lenses when the Good Lord specifically designed the eyeball to expel foreign objects, and wasn't she tempting fate and physiology? And she smiles serenely and says, "But with glasses I feel like a candidate for euthanasia."

Superwoman

Every once in a while Ralph wonders out loud why it is that I've never made anything of myself.

I've never quite been able to convince Ralph that this kind of statement is not conducive to increasing one's confidence. From time to time, even, it has made me contemplate standing on the ledge of the Coronado Bay Bridge with a loaded diaper pail pointed at my head.

Ralph, I should mention, also likes to have me home when he gets there at night and prefers it if I can be available when he has a morning or afternoon off.

"I think what you're trying to say," I said to Ralph at one point, "is that you'd like me to have a demanding but satisfying, well-paying, high-status job tailor-made to your erratic working hours."

"Well," said Ralph, "is that too much to ask?"

It's not that Ralph regards me as a failure—just "between successes." I have tried several times to convey to him that I do not personally perceive my current life as simply a holding pattern—that there might be some inherent value in motherhood and home management.

Ralph couldn't agree more. That's why he is adamant that the demanding but satisfying, well-paying, high-status job should be no more than half-time.

Actually, I suspect that Ralph's remarks would not bother me if part of me didn't agree with him. I should mention here that I come from an achievement-oriented background where women were strongly encouraged to have careers. My grandmother had a Ph.D. in zoology. Even my great-grandmother graduated from college, in 1880.

If I were *really* confident in my position, I'd shake my head sadly at Ralph and explain that it was *his* problem if he had trouble seeing people in any but their career identities (which is, after all, only one of many facets of a person) and point out how fortunate it was that at least one of us was not hampered by such a narrow view of humanity.

Unfortunately, I'm not that confident. A lot of the time, of course, I go on with my day-to-day life as a mother, working harder than I ever worked when I was "working," and on many days, I genuinely regard it as a pleasant and bona fide stage of my life — not just an interlude or a time-out from a "real" career. How, I ask myself, can a job as important as child care be so undervalued?

But then, just before I fall asleep at night, a little voice in my head pipes up. "Hey, Louise," it says, "how come you've never made anything of yourself?"

A child's garden of complex issues

" 'Old Mother Hubbard went to the cupboard, to get her poor dog a bone. And — ' "

"Why, Mommy?"

"Why? Well, I guess she thought it would be a nice treat for the dog."

"Why?"

"Well, I imagine Old Mother Hubbard was a kind lady who liked animals — "

"Why?"

"Well, people often do nice things for other people and animals, just because it makes them feel good."

"Why?"

"Well, it's important for people to have a sense of cooperation, of helping each other if there's ever going to be world peace. As I was saying, she knew dogs liked bones — "

"Why?"

"Well, they just do. Just the way little boys like cookies. The bone is kind of like a cookie for the dog. He chews on it with his teeth and it makes him feel good."

"Why?"

"I don't know. Maybe it releases endorphins in his brain or something. This is not Mommy's strong field. The point is—"

"Where she get the doggie?"

"Well, it doesn't say exactly. Probably she had a neighbor with a large litter and they gave her one of the puppies."

"We call Mother Hubber? Ask her?"

"Since you mention it, it's also possible she got it from the ASPCA. That's a group of people who really like animals and want to help them. You see, we can't actually call Old Mother Hubbard because she is not a real person. This is just a story."

"Why?"

"Well, nice people write stories so that little boys like Alan have something fun to read before they go to bed."

"Why she not real?"

"It's possible that at one time she was real. That there was actually somebody named Old Mother Hubbard who had a dog and somebody wrote about her. Mommy doesn't know for sure."

"Why?"

"Well, because Mommy doesn't know everything."

"Why?"

"Well, because there's more to know in the world than any one person can possibly learn."

"Why?"

"Well, because the world is such a big and complicated place. Let's finish the story. 'When she got there, the cupboard was bare—'"

"Why?"

"She may have forgotten to go to Safeway, or maybe she was poor and didn't have enough money to buy food."

"Why?"

"Well, you see, some people can't find jobs so they can earn money to buy food."

"Why?"

"Well, because of inflation, recession, soaring interest rates. I think this is getting a little over your head. Most likely, Old Mother Hubbard was a very nice little old lady who was a little short of money the day the story was written, but the next day was going to get some money from some nice people named Social Security, who make sure little old ladies and their doggies have enough to eat. Then she was going to go out and buy a whole cupboardful of groceries for herself and a bunch of nice, juicy bones for the dog. So even though it seems like a sad story, we can imagine that it had a happy ending. Here's Daddy to say goodnight. Sweetheart, can you tell Daddy why Old Mother Hubbard went to get her poor dog a bone?"

"He was hungry."

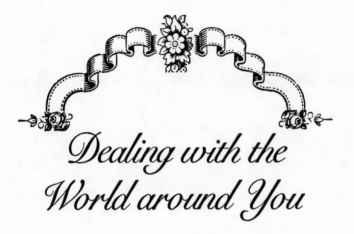

Dealing with the
World around You

In previous generations, marriage partners generally experienced a far more limited contact with the rest of the world than their counterparts in today's complex society. Increased mobility, rapidly developing technology, and changing mores have all served to expose the couple to an array of influences, choices, and institutions that would have been unheard of by their forebears and that complicate relationships even with such traditional associates as friends, relatives, and neighbors.

While the institution of marriage can be a welcome refuge from the pressures of society, a couple still must face the task of coming to grips with the world around them.

This provides for some interesting experiences.

Moral issues

Up until twenty years ago, things were very clear. Nudity was a state of undress, moral when employed in the procreation of children, or in great works of art before 1750. Perversity was two or more nude bodies of the same sex not in a locker room, or three nude bodies, mixed sexes, anywhere. Masturbation was a filthy, depraved act that grew hair on your palms and was responsible for the meteoric rise of the depilatory industry. Now nothing is clear. It's no wonder young people are a little confused.

For example, I remember very clearly that when I reached adolescence, the Big Question was whether you should let a guy kiss you on the first date. We talked about it endlessly in hygiene class and Girl Scouts and they always implied that if you did, you would probably be on your way to a home for unwed mothers by the time you were fourteen.

And just as I was getting all that straight in my head, I go off to college where the Big Question was whether or not you should *sleep* with the guy on the first date. Now this was a major change in theoretical orientation, not to mention topography, and just as I'm deciding where I stand on that, the Big Question was suddenly how long you should wait before telling your folks you were living with someone (even if you weren't).

You didn't have to *do* any of these things, of course, but you did have to make some decisions about them and reconcile your own moral upbringing with what everybody else in the dorm was doing. (Everybody else in the dorm was defined as two or more people who looked like they were having a lot more fun than you.) This often caused intense internal turmoil.

Well, just as you think you have it all together, you get married and go to graduate school about the time the women's movement is gaining momentum and suddenly everybody in your women's group is asking, What's a nice way to tell him you want to be on top? After that, it seemed like there was a new Big Question every five weeks instead of every five years, and the questions started getting incredibly complex and specialized, involving preferences and paraphernalia heretofore unacknowledged by sex-education books.

In all fairness, it couldn't have been easy being a parent during these times either. It seems to be that even the "old school" parents are getting a little cynical about morality these days. Take my dad, for example, a staunchly conservative person. He and I were watching the Olympic games on TV one year, the ones where they paraded out the eighty girls in white who were supposed to be Vestal Virgins. And Dad looked at them and said drily, "I wonder where they found eighty of them."

In-laws: The third visit

As they said in my assertiveness-training class, why suffer in silence when a few simple words to the right person can solve your problem? Sounded easy enough, but they had clearly never dealt with someone like Ralph's father.

Don't get me wrong. I love Pop. He is generous, witty, scrupulously honest. And stubborn as forty-six constipated oxen.

He would not, for example, change his watch to our time, persisting instead in maintaining for an entire two-week visit an eating and sleeping schedule three hours different from ours. (This was not a hostess's dream.)

He naturally got up three hours earlier than the rest of the household but kindly made a large pot of coffee for when the rest of us got up. Unfortunately, it was always much too weak. An easily correctable problem, however.

LOUISE Pop, I know you're not used to our coffee maker, everybody's is different and all, but you need to put in more coffee. It's a little weak.
POP The problem is you're using the wrong grind. Gotta use perk.
LOUISE Perk doesn't work with a drip coffee maker, Pop.
POP The problem is you gotta use drip then. By the way, the Ipso Facto wants out.
LOUISE The dog is a Lhasa apso, Pop, and you know it. We've always used regular grind and it works just fine. You're just not using enough of it.
POP So maybe it gets weaker by the time you late risers get up.
LOUISE It does not get weaker and we get up at seven A.M. Look, Pop, it's not a question of anyone being right or wrong.

˙You just need to put in more coffee. You'll do that?

POP   The problem is your filters are too heavy. Makes it too weak.

LOUISE   There is nothing wrong with our filters, Pop. I just hate to throw out a whole pot of coffee because it's not strong enough, that's all.

POP   Must be something wrong with this brand of coffee. *(Glances at watch.)* Looks like it's getting to be time for lunch.

LOUISE   IT IS EIGHT-THIRTY IN THE MORNING AND IT IS NOT TIME FOR LUNCH. Look, Pop, why don't you just change your watch to our time, get up when we get up, and I'll make the coffee. Will you do that? Just say yes or no.

POP   The problem is your coffee maker's no good.

LOUISE   THERE IS NOTHING WRONG WITH OUR COFFEE MAKER OR OUR COFFEE. YOU JUST NEED MORE COFFEE. DO YOU HEAR ME?

RALPH   *(entering)* What's everyone yelling about?

POP   I was just telling Louise she's got some problems with her coffee maker and she got hysterical.

LOUISE   *(weeping softly into her cereal)* I can't cope anymore, Ralph.

POP   I think the Ipso Facto wants in.

Crime

Ralph and I are very security conscious.

Houseguests have remarked on occasion that they think it's a terrific idea to need a key to get into a house, but that it seems excessive to need one to get out again. (What can you say to a guest who has been inadvertently double dead-bolted into your house for two hours and tried to get out through a window, only to discover after considerable effort that none of them can be forced up more than six inches? You can say you'll pay for his herniorrhaphy, that's what.)

The reason for all these precautions, of course, is that during the first two years of our marriage, Ralph and I were burgled five times.

It got so that every time we came home, we'd get into an argument about whose turn it was to call the police and whose turn it was to fill out the insurance forms.

It even got to the point that whenever someone we knew was burgled, their instantaneous reaction was not to call the police but to call Ralph and Louise. It's as if they just associated the words "rip-off" and "DeGrave." We've aided so many people in dealing with their burglaries that we've considered starting a nationwide self-help group, Ravaged Anonymous.

We tried to keep the burglars out, but frankly, the neighborhood was lousy and the condition of our rental house even lousier. We put in floodlights. Double dead-bolt locks. We even nailed down the windows in August.

It was when we started leaving notes for the burglars that we knew we were desperate.

Dear Burglars:

I'm posting this on your favorite window so you'll see it. Just answer me one question. Why would any burglar with all his marbles keep breaking into a house with homemade furniture (which our friends charitably describe as "Early American two-by-four") and a bank book on the kitchen table with $1.72 in it? You could do better.

Also, you missed the unwanted wedding gifts last time. They are in that built-in cupboard in the dining alcove in a drawer marked (for your convenience) "Unwanted Wedding Gifts." I agree that some of the stuff, like that candlesnuffer, should just be put out of its misery, but we'd consider it a special favor if you'd take it. You owe us one.

Dear Burglars:

I don't think you are playing fair about this at all. If you're going to hit up the TV, the least you could do is take the (unwanted) wedding gifts. (It wouldn't hurt you to be a little neater either.)

We are not going to replace the TV or any small appliance again until further notice. We mean that! So don't bother coming back to get the replacement.

Go pick on somebody rich!

Dear Burglars:

Happy New Year! Is it possible your fence has an outlet for neckties?

This month we are having a special on accessories — the case to the typewriter, the manual for the TV set, the cord to the fry pan, etc. (That was a rotten trick, taking the fry pan. There is such a thing as basic human dignity.) They are in a drawer above Unwanted Wedding Gifts (hint) marked "Remnants of Ripped-Offables."

Dear Burglars:

Well, this is good-bye. We're moving. There is no forwarding address.

I hope you won't think I'm being too familiar if I offer you some parting advice, but after all, you've been over here more than most of our friends.

The police keep telling us you're pros. So act like it! Take those Gant shirts of my husband's for example. (You already have.) They were irregulars from the outlet place in the Bronx, you ninnies: $3.50 each new.

So maybe you got $.50 each for them (less for the ones with only one sleeve and "DeGrave — No Starch" written in the collar.) For maybe $6.00, you'd risk getting sent up?

That's all I wanted to say. Well, I guess, as the saying goes, it's been real.

Fortunately, we had insurance. I had taken out a tenant's policy only fifteen days before the first burgle, over Ralph's rabid objections.

"But, Louise," he said at the time, "what do we need insurance for? We have just moved *away* from crime-ridden New York. We are now living in the friendly Midwest."

We'd never been burgled once in crime-ridden New York. Funny thing about the friendly Midwest.

Anyway, by the time the burglars were done with us, we were reduced to owning a house full of neo-penal-style furniture and a bunch of junk even a burglar couldn't love. Strangely, it was almost a relief.

"Do you realize," said Ralph one day, "that we have nothing

left to steal? We can open the windows in the summertime again. We have nothing left to fear."

Of course, freedom from fear had its inconveniences. Ralph, who has a very sensitive musical ear, was reduced to listening to AM, which is all the car radio had. It was a fate worse than death as far as he was concerned.

And for the two months it took for the insurance money to come in after his clothes were stolen, poor Ralph used to get up every morning and fling open his empty closet where his one pathetic suit and shirt were hanging and inquire good-naturedly, "Well, what shall I wear today?"

And then, I'll never forget him sitting out in the car at the curb in a raging blizzard with his blanket and can of beer listening to a football game.

It also gave us an opportunity to get to know our local law-enforcement officers, a group we continue not to hold in high esteem. Every time we got hit, they'd send around this turkey-ball detective who would hand us a card with a case number on it and earnestly assure us, "Let us know if you get any leads on your case."

"I thought that was supposed to be our line," Ralph said drily.

On the positive side, however, it is very easy to move when you don't own anything. But when we got to our new home, we made the fatal mistake: We started Acquiring again.

One day, not long after the move, Ralph came home with a stereo. "We can afford it," he said defensively.

"But Ralph," I said, "the stereo is the least of it. Can we afford dead-bolt locks on the doors, special deterrents on sixteen windows, and timers on lights that go off at the most awkward social moments? Do we want to go back to wondering who's going to rip off the stereo, to not opening the door for Boy Scouts selling light bulbs? Is it worth it to us, Ralph? Is it?"

Ralph plugged in the stereo, attached some wires, switched it to FM, and listened for a few minutes.

"Yes," he said finally, a mellow look spreading across his face, "it's worth it."

(What you'll do for) Good friends

We love animals, we really do. In times past, they have lived in our house, slept in our bed, and eaten off our plates. Some of our best friends are animals.

Though we had no pets of our own for several years of our marriage, we perennially had a vacationing friend's pet in residence. So we didn't hesitate to volunteer to keep Lassie, a full-grown (we hoped) eight-month-old golden retriever, while her "parents" vacationed. (Afterward we thought we understood why they needed to go.)

"No problem," I assured Lassie's mother, Linda, as I walked her to the front door. "We have a fenced yard, we love animals, and Lassie'll adore us."

"By the way," said Linda, "she's still in kind of a chewy stage, so don't leave things lying around. And don't let her into the house. She leaps over sofas in a single bound."

By the time I got back to Lassie, she had eaten her leash, our plastic watering can, and a whole box of dog treats.

The leash was just an apertif. During the next two weeks, Lassie also consumed a twenty-five-pound bag of dry dog chow, which reappeared with almost lightning speed (and in seemingly identical form) as Lassie-doo, which Ralph went around collecting with great martyrdom in a plastic bucket twice a day.

"We're only taking small dogs from now on," he grumbled, hauling the afternoon's installment to the pile along the far corner of the back fence. The man who mowed the lawn refused to touch the backyard, even with Lassie incarcerated in the bathroom eating the bath mat. ("No work. Stink," he said when I tried to persuade him.)

For a while we thought we were overfeeding her, so we tried

cutting out her evening meal. When we came out the next morning, she had devoured eight potted plants, some down to the root balls.

"Do you think any of the plants were poisonous?" I inquired anxiously.

"There's always hope," muttered Ralph.

We even tried training her in the brief time she was with us. "Bad dog!" said Ralph when he caught Lassie chewing through the garden hoses. Lassie looked at Ralph nervously and backed away, knocking the potted Christmas tree off the front porch into the bushes.

Three days before Departure Day, we came home to find that Lassie had emptied the contents of two full garbage cans over the entire backyard. While I scraped vegetable peelings off the patio, Ralph leaned on his shovel, ankle deep in coffee grounds, and said, "This is a dog only its owner could love."

"Any problems?" said Linda when she came to pick up Lassie.

"Not a thing," said Ralph as Lassie stood there slobbering on Ralph's pant leg. "Such a nice dog."

"What happened to your plants?" said Linda nervously.

"Locusts," said Ralph.

(What you'd like to do to) Not-so-good friends

One year during the holiday season, we hosted a small dinner party. After an hour and forty-eight minutes, however, one of the guests still hadn't arrived. I eventually concluded that he'd been in a tragic automobile accident and couldn't call. Tears filled my eyes. Poor Fred. But I knew he'd want us all to eat, so I finally served up the dried-out, warmed-over supper I'd been holding.

"Hi, everybody, sorry I'm late," said Fred breathlessly when he arrived a few minutes later. "I just couldn't get in gear today."

"Louise," said my husband Ralph politely, "why don't you take Fred's coat?"

"No, Ralph, you go," I whispered demurely. "If I get anywhere near Fred, he'll be a soprano for life."

For some reason, party invitations seem to bring out the most boorish behavior in some individuals. This phenomenon was especially evident at a party at my friend Charlotte's house that we went to several weeks after our own.

Now, Charlotte had what I thought was a reasonable turnout at her party, but as witnessed by the remaining thirteen covered dishes in the refrigerator, not nearly what she was expecting.

"Hello, so nice of you to come," said Charlotte, pumping my hand automatically and fixing me with glazed eyes and a frozen smile when I came into the kitchen.

"Charlotte," I said, "it's me, Louise."

Charlotte's smile suddenly thawed as she indicated all the covered dishes with a wave of her hand. "I am *never* having another party again," she said.

"Why don't we take all the leftovers and mail them in plain brown wrappers to all the guests who didn't show up?" I said.

"Where did I go wrong?" said Charlotte, scooping an uneaten five-quart casserole into the cat's dish. "Only twenty people even responded to the invitation. Does no answer mean yes or no? Even the people who answered didn't say they were actually coming," she continued, packing the casserole into the cat's dish with her foot. "They all said they'd 'drop by.' " We watched the cat licking the top off the casserole with gusto. " 'Drop by'! I wanted to say, 'Don't do me any favors!' "

"You wouldn't think it was that big a commitment," I agreed.

"In the town where I grew up, people seemed to take responsibility for their own good time," said Charlotte, picking up bits of casserole that had fallen on the floor and tucking them back into the cat's dish. "Now they show up two hours late, and if the party's not in full swing, they say it's boring and leave!"

I nodded my head.

"I just don't know whether I should take it personally," continued Charlotte, "or decide that some people are just insensitive, like your friend Fred."

At that moment, the doorbell rang.

"Hi, Charlotte," said the young woman at the door. "I completely lost track of the time. I hope it's not too late to get something to eat. I'm starving!"

"No, not at all, Vivian," said Charlotte, as she surreptitiously scooped casserole out of the cat's dish onto a plate. "A glass of wine, perhaps?"

Pornographic movies

For our anniversary, Ralph and I and our friends Stan and Susan intended to have a nice dinner and see "The Man Who Would Be King." The dinner, however, took longer than expected and the theater was sold out by the time we got there. So we decided to try the movie next door, which turned out to be a pornographic film about a guy with arrested emotional development. (Ralph dubbed it "The Man Who Would Be Queen.")

It was my first triple-X-rated movie and I was frankly ready for a little erotica.

The entire plot of this movie was developed during the first and last one-and-a-half minutes. The first sexual act didn't begin, however, until we were a full 170 seconds into the film. ("They're just teasing us," said Stan, explaining the delay.) In addition to the "hero," there were five other basic characters, and every combination and permutation was, shall we say, executed.

Before I go further on the relative merits of the film, I learned a valuable lesson about pornographic movies. That is, never take off your coat in the middle of the movie, or people behind you might misinterpret your actions and say suggestive things loud enough for you to hear them, such that your husband will want to punch them out. Do not fold it up in your lap either.

On the positive side, I'd have to say that the movie was technically well done, considering the difficult angles and lighting situations.

There were even attempts at symbolism. Every time the "heroine" walked by the butler, the camera cut back to burning embers in the fireplace. ("Heavy," said Ralph.)

When the heroine and the butler actually got together, the camera cut back to the embers bursting into flame. ("Deep," said Stan.)

On the negative side, I'd have to say that interpersonal sanitary conditions in this film were deplorable.

You also needed a sharp eye and a cooperative effort to keep up with the characters. The camera kept introducing new scenes with just torsos, no heads. ("Who's that?" said Stan at one point. "It's the butler, of course," said Susan.)

I have to say that one reaches a saturation point very quickly.

"They must have had a no-cut contract," yawned Ralph toward the end as he munched M&M's from the large, economy-sized bag we had brought with us.

"Tell Ralph to pass the M&M's if he has a free hand," said Stan.

I inquired as to when it might be over.

"Well," said Stan, who had seen a number of these movies before, "they've still got at least ten minutes, and let's see, we haven't had the butler do it to the hero, the butler and the maid do it to the best friend, or a group bondage number."

"They're going to do all that in ten minutes?" I said.

"Sure, loads of time," said Stan. And they did.

Since pornographic movies are often linked to a certain impulsivity, I was curious about Ralph's reaction to it.

"Tell me," I said as we were leaving the theater, "does watching a movie like that make you want to assault the first woman you see?"

Ralph thought for a minute. "No," he said finally. "But I might be interested in a pizza."

The mathematics of social interaction: A little quiz

Problem #1: Logistics

Given: (a) Three couples, all with (b) small children, who live in (c) different areas of the city, want to (d) get together at a (e) restaurant that has food that (f) everyone likes, (g) no one is allergic to, (h) has a children's menu, (i) is preferably gourmet, and (j) has two or more high chairs, (l) tolerates children, but is (m) not too noisy, and is (n) centrally located (o) not more than ten miles' driving distance from any one couple's home, and (p) opens at 5 P.M., (q) has a table big enough for all of you if they don't take reservations, (r) assuming, of course, that Couple No. 2 can (s) find a sitter who (t) is available at such an early hour and (u) is willing to take care of kids with chicken pox and (v) doesn't get a last-minute date to the junior prom which is the same night, and that (w) the weather holds up, and (x) nobody's car breaks down, and (y) the kids behave, the question is, (z) is it worth it?

Problem #2: Set Theory

Your husband casually mentions at breakfast that it might be fun to get together with someone this weekend. After he has gone to work, the Smiths coincidentally call and invite you for dinner Saturday night. Won't your husband be pleased!

Oops! Your husband arrives home and announces that he ran into the Petersons over his lunch hour and invited them here for dinner Saturday.

Phooey! You'd rather go to the Smiths since you like them

very much, not to mention they'll have to cook instead of you. Besides which, that invitation was made first.

No way! Your husband insists it would be in extremely poor taste to invite the Petersons to your home for dinner and cancel for anything other than a dire emergency. Briefly, you consider inviting the Smiths over on Saturday night along with the Petersons, but reject this idea. (If the Smiths really like you, and the Petersons really like you, why did the Smiths and the Petersons hate each other at your last dinner party? Correct answer will receive Nobel Peace Prize.)

Embarrassed, you call the Smiths, who fortunately say, "No problem, let's make it Sunday night instead." All's well that ends well.

Darn! The next night the Smiths call back and say that her mother is coming out Sunday. So much for the free meal.

Having gotten all revved up to go out Sunday, you say what the heck and call the Harrises, inviting them to go to the movies with you. They accept.

Oh, no! An hour later, the Smiths call back. Her mother might not come on Sunday after all. They're not sure yet.

Not wanting the Smiths to know you made other plans so soon (how were you to know?), having already changed plans with them once, you call the Harrises back, apologize profusely, and ask if the following Sunday would be OK.

Damn! The next day the Smiths call back. Her mother is definitely coming Sunday.

Shit! The Petersons call. He threw his back out and they'll have to cancel.

That weekend you: (choose one or more)

a. Socialize Saturday and Sunday
b. Socialize Saturday but not Sunday
c. Socialize Sunday but not Saturday
d. Socialize neither Saturday nor Sunday
e. Decide to join a monastery
f. Go out for pizza

Problem #3: Combinations and Permutations

If for two couples to be good friends, it is necessary that you like her husband and your husband likes her husband, and her husband likes your husband, and your husband likes her, and she likes you, and she likes your husband, and you like her, and her husband likes you, what is the probability of married couples ever forming close attachments?

Neighbors

One positive thing you can say for disasters is that they are frequently a good way to get to know the neighbors.

Ralph and I first learned this when we bought our first house (in Colorado) and, one week later, accidentally set it on fire.

Actually, "we" didn't set it on fire; Ralph did. As he admitted later, "I guess you never know how hot an electric stove can get until you put three quarts of french-fry oil on a burner and forget about it."

It fortunately wasn't a serious fire, thanks, of course, to the fire department. It scorched one wall and left the back door rather on the charred side.

Of course, before the fire, we'd been meaning to go out and meet the neighbors, particularly the ones next door. But our evenings had always been occupied with unpacking boxes and building bookcases — which was exactly what Ralph was doing when he forgot about the oil.

Frankly, I've never quite forgiven Ralph for his timing. At the moment the kitchen ignited, I happened to be off wombing in the shower, trying to recover from a very hard day at work. Just as I was getting into some very pleasant fetal memories, Ralph comes charging in yelling, "Fire!" (It was my fastest rebirth on record.)

Heart in mouth, I grabbed my pink quilted bathrobe — the ratty one with only one button left and the fallen hem — that I'd gotten when I was twelve, and while Ralph rounded up the cat and dog, I went dashing over to the next-door neighbors' and began pounding on their door.

Did I mention it was twenty-two degrees and snowing?

I don't need to say that the expression on the face of the neighbors' teenage son when he opened the door and saw a dripping-wet stranger standing barefoot in the snow clutching a ratty pink bathrobe around her was one of surprise.

"I'm-your-new-neighbor-Quick!-Call-the-fire-department-our-house-is-on-fire!" I blurted breathlessly.

"Oh, sure! Right away!" Before I could say another word, he had slammed the front door shut and rushed toward the phone where I could hear him urgently talking to the operator as I stood on the porch, freezing to death.

For dramatic quality, there's nothing like four fire engines screeching to a halt in front of your house to bring the neighbors out in droves. Quickly, the firemen extinguished the blaze and began to disperse the thick smoke in the house with huge fans.

Well, there we are standing in the snow and dark, the cat and dog and I (in the ratty bathrobe) and Ralph (who later turns out to be in partial shock, having suffered second-degree burns from mid-thigh to ankle after initially having tried to put out the fire himself), and we're thanking God we're safe, and watching smoke billow out our front door, and wondering how serious the damage will be, and suddenly someone is tapping us on the shoulder.

"Hi! You must be the new neighbors. Name's Tom Hammond. My wife, Jean. Looks like you folks are having a little trouble here." (As we're blinded by flashing lights from the four fire trucks and the police car that has since arrived.) "Nothing serious, I hope?"

Well, next thing we know, there's all these people milling around our front yard chatting with each other and introducing themselves to us.

Well, after that incident, we just seemed to be part of the

neighborhood. There is something about sharing a disaster, or even a potential one, with your neighbors that instantly puts you on a first-name basis.

Next time we bought a house, however, we just had a cocktail party.

Now, when you buy a home, there's a certain number of unknowns you can never predict ahead of time. All kinds of things can happen. Belatedly you discover that the neighbor's dog barks all night or that a superhighway is going to be routed through your backyard or that the house next door doubles as a massage parlor. Well, our house didn't have any of those problems. What we couldn't have predicted ahead of time, however, were the next-door neighbors.

I mean, they couldn't have been nicer people, Granny and Grampy and their daughter Edna and their grandson the Jesus freak. It's just that they had this way of invading your life all the time.

Take the grandson, for example. A terrifically nice kid and all, but he had this habit of showing up on our doorstep, Bible in hand, five minutes after we got home at night and inquiring, "Mrs. DeGrave, have you ever met . . . Him?"

"Him who?" I remember saying the first time. (From the way he said it, I began to worry that the Boston Strangler had been paroled and was living down the block. In the neighborhood we were living, this was entirely possible.)

"Him," he repeated, a little piqued that "him" could be anyone but "Him."

"Oh, *Him*," I said, getting the idea, finally.

This family was very security conscious (and Ralph and I thought *we* were bad) and had installed a burglar alarm wired not only to the front and back doors and all the windows, but to the inside closet doors as well, in case someone should get in by some other entrance than the above. When activated, this alarm set off not only an ear-piercing siren that could be heard for four miles, but a flashing red beacon mounted on top of the chimney.

That was OK except that the family tended to get up at five-thirty every morning and, in their sleepy state, open closet doors. Without deactivating the alarm.

The first time it happened, Ralph and I nearly had a heart attack. Five-thirty in the morning and suddenly we're blasted out of bed by this siren and there's this flashing red light revolving in our bedroom (the two houses were only ten feet apart). Instantly we hit the floor, convinced the police had the place surrounded.

Well, this would occur about three or four times per week and gradually we almost got used to it. Although, I have to say, you had to have a strong heart to live in our house.

As I said before, they were very nice people even when their grandson was converting the Jesus into us and their siren was scaring the bejeezus out of us, and one of the nicest things from our point of view was that Granny, a really dear old lady, spent most of her time sitting at her front window looking out at the world — and our house.

"Built-in security!" said Ralph excitedly when we first moved in. We were both gone all day and had only bought this house to get away from our rental on Burglary Row. The new neighborhood was a little better, certainly. But not that much better.

So imagine Ralph's astonishment when he comes home one night and there's the garage door open and this teenage kid is in the process of ripping off the (new) stereo. Well, the kid takes off rather rapidly, Ralph in hot pursuit, but the kid got away (fortunately, empty-handed).

Well, just as Ralph is arriving breathlessly back at the house, I arrive and we both notice Granny waving at us from her window.

"Granny," I said, "did you see anything? Ralph just caught a kid trying to rob our house!"

"Aha!" said Granny. "I thought so! When I saw that boy going in through your garage a while back, I said to myself, 'I wonder if the DeGraves are being robbed?' " Granny cackled to herself in delight, clearly pleased with her deductive acumen. "Wait'll I tell Edna!"

Ralph looked at me and I looked at him.

"We'll get twenty years for killing an old lady," said Ralph finally.

"Yeah," I said, and we went home.

Car salesmen

At 34,000 miles our Vega was fast biting the dust, and in a moment of truth, Ralph and I decided that it simply had to go. Of course, when Ralph's bus-riding career failed, we were then faced with finding a replacement. After two long days of talking to car dealers, we wearily ended up back at the place where we'd been offered the best deal.

SALESMAN *(acting shocked with disbelief)* The salesman you talked to yesterday offered to discount this car four hundred dollars from the sticker and you — you — you want *more?*

RALPH That's right.

SALESMAN Ralph, I'm telling ya. This ain't no charity. *(To me)* And how old's that sweet little baby?

LOUISE *(wearily)* Twenty-six. He's just small for his age.

SALESMAN Well, Ralph, I'll write this up and we'll just pray this is your lucky day and the manager goes for it. Let's see, you want to walk out the door for five thousand, so working back, six percent on five thousand gives us a base price of —

RALPH No, that's wrong. You calculate the tax from the base price, not the total price. The total price includes the tax.

Forty minutes later

SALESMAN Ralph, I just don't understand this system of yours at all. I've been selling cars twenty-five years and I've always figured the tax my way.

LOUISE *(with sudden sinking feeling)* I think I want to leave, Ralph.

SALESMAN OK, we'll forget the tax for now. Let's see, we've got ninety-one dollars for the license, one-fifty for the radio —

RALPH Hold it! I thought we agreed on one-twenty for the radio.

SALESMAN You sure drive a hard bargain, Ralph. All right, I'll give you the radio for one-twenty. But I'm losing money on it.

RALPH The salesman yesterday said that one-twenty was the regular, already-jacked-up price.

SALESMAN New guy. Doesn't know the business yet. You want a luggage rack?

RALPH That's supposed to come with it. It's right here in the picture in your ad.

SALESMAN That's a mistake. It's eighty dollars extra.

RALPH That's false advertising!

SALESMAN Oh, now, Ralph. Let's not get to name-calling.

RALPH I want to talk to the manager.

Ten minutes later

MANAGER They accidentally ran a picture of the wrong car. We were *very* upset when we saw it. But tell you folks what. To give you a break, that rack usually costs one-twenty. We'll let you have it for sixty. And we're losing money on the deal.

LOUISE You sure lose a lot of money around here.

RALPH Do not feed the lions, Louise.

MANAGER To folks like you, tough customers, we end up givin' cars away. Don't make a dime. Just like to see people going away happy.

RALPH Except that your salesman said the rack was eighty dollars, full price.

MANAGER New guy. Doesn't know the business yet. *(Sincere look)* Folks, I'm talking to you straight. I'd rather lose the deal than sell a car to folks who didn't think I was honest.

LOUISE *(whispering to Ralph)* Shall we throw up now or later?

SALESMAN *(entering manager's office)* Got this offer all writ up for you folks, if you'll just step outside. *(To us)* Start praying!

RALPH *(to Louise)* Let's throw up now.

SALESMAN *(returning)* Folks, he says he just can't do it. He'd be —

LOUISE   Don't tell me. "Losing money on the deal."
SALESMAN   How'd you know?
LOUISE   I think I'm beginning to know the business.

Modern Medicine

Looking at my calendar one morning, I realized it was time for
me to go in for a routine one-year follow-up visit for the
surgery I'd had the year before. So I called the hospital
out-patient clinic for an appointment.

"Do you have insurance?" inquired the receptionist.

"Oh, I'm an old patient," I assured her. "I've been there
dozens of times."

"Oh, I know," she said patiently. "What I meant was, do you
still have insurance?"

I actually couldn't believe she wouldn't have given me an
appointment even if I hadn't had insurance, but I had barely
sat down at my desk again when the phone rang and it was the
hospital insurance office. They wanted to *confirm* that I still had
insurance.

Of course, I offered to have my insurance carrier call them
personally, but they said that wasn't necessary. They did,
however, ask that I come in a half hour early to sign some
forms at the admitting office.

Admitting office? "I think you are under the mistaken
impression I'm being admitted," I said. "Actually, I'm just
coming in for a routine visit to the clinic. No tests, even." (No
wonder they were so uptight about the insurance.)

"Oh, we know," she said. She also mentioned that I would be
receiving a packet of forms to fill out in the near future.

The near future, as it turned out, was the next morning. A
map to the hospital, a medical-history checklist, several pages
of detailed billing information, and an insurance data sheet
arrived, all encased in a nice cardboard jacket with a cover
photo of a rapturously happy patient being adoringly cared for
by the hospital staff. On the back was another photo, this one a

white-coated type fondling some very complex gismo full of test tubes containing what looked like blood. (The centrifuged remains of patients who didn't have insurance?)

I don't know what it was that made me feel this way, but at this point I started to get nervous. I got even more nervous when I began filling out the insurance data sheet. My policy number and next of kin I didn't mind telling them, but what did they need with the next of kin's occupation? Or the name and address of the nearest relative not living with me? (That, of course, was my dad.)

Now, normally I would have been glad to impart this information without question, but all of a sudden I found myself wanting to know why *they* wanted to know. Could they make Dad pay up if Ralph and I and the insurance company all reneged? If he wouldn't, could they come take away his car? His house? God forbid, Dad himself?

Really, I told myself, you're getting paranoid.

So I put that form aside and moved on to the next three sheets in the pile: a document making me financially responsible for all charges, regardless. A warning that if my insurer didn't pay up in forty-five days, I was responsible for the entire bill. And a notice that even with insurance, outpatients were required to put down a $100 deposit. (For No Insurance: a $250 deposit, and pay the balance on your way out.)

So I read all that, then casually flipped back to the insurance form. Next to "nearest relative not living with you" I wrote, "None. (Orphan.)"

The morning of my appointment, I duly went to Admissions with my packet of forms, all neatly filed in the cardboard jacket with the photos of the ecstatic patient and the centrifuged uninsureds. There I signed three more forms: two more financial agreements and a release of information to my insurer.

The doctor, by the way, said I was fine.

Family Planning,
Part 2: Birth

During times of stress, marriage partners tend to resort to characteristic coping styles. The months pre- and postchildbirth, for example, pose particular difficulties for each member of the family. The wife is frequently forced to give up some of her own needs for nurturing in favor of the nurturing needs of the child. The overwhelming physical and emotional demands of her new situation may leave her little time for her husband, causing a major disruption in the previous balance of the marital relationship. The husband may find it especially difficult to tolerate this psychological absence, feeling ostracized and abandoned by his wife. In the case of the birth of a second child, the older sibling often views the newborn as a rival for his mother's love and attention, and may act out his turmoil in a variety of what his parents perceive as objectionable ways.

Ultimately, the family needs to be flexible enough to switch from the normal mother-child symbiosis to a family system in which the husband-wife bond regains priority.

In the meantime, however, it's chaos.

Pregnancy, and other surprises

Most of our long-term friends have been able to count on two things: the sun would come up tomorrow, and Louise would never get pregnant.

It's a funny thing. After nine childless years and an adoption, nobody dares ask if you're pregnant, even if it's your eighth month and you're standing there at a cocktail party with your wineglass and a plate of hors d'oeuvres balanced on your stomach. (Not that I blame them; in their circumstances, I wouldn't have asked me if I was pregnant either.) Instead, they'll just sort of stand there, shifting uncomfortably from one foot to the other, sneaking glances at your stomach, and inquiring brightly, "Well, what's new?"

Now, I will unabashedly admit that I loved being pregnant. I think God was feeling sorry for me by that time, as I never suffered from nausea, leg cramps, heartburn, swollen hands and feet, or any of the other discomforts pregnancy is known for. Indeed, the only real suffering I endured during my pregnancy was nine months of people telling me, "That always happens after you adopt."

By my fourth month, this phrase was beginning to drive me cumulatively wild. First of all, it doesn't "always happen." It just always *seems* like it always happens. And in my case, it didn't "just happen" at all.

A long (three years), painful (all manner of gruesome tests), and expensive (you wouldn't believe) investigation revealed that the source of my infertility was a small, benign pituitary tumor, which ultimately required two surgeries to remove. (For details, send $7.95 for my cassette recording, "How I Suffered," and its sequel, "How I Suffered Some More.") After the second one, I got pregnant almost immediately. Nine years, $20,000, two brain surgeries, and people tell me it "always happens." It's enough to make you weep.

Progressive parents that we were, Ralph and I set about preparing Alan for the new arrival. Since Alan was just beginning to express an interest in comparative anatomy, this seemed an ideal time to begin his sex education.

For reasons still unknown to us, Alan always chose to review this information when we were stuck in a long supermarket checkout line, invariably scandalizing some sweet little old lady who had made the fatal mistake of commenting to Alan about the baby in Mommy's tummy.

"It's not in her tummy," Alan would protest. "It's in her *uterus.*" (A supermarket can be so noisy you can't think straight until a two-year-old says "uterus." Then you can hear a pin drop.) "And it's going to come out her vagina! Do you have a uterus too?"

(One poor elderly lady pointedly said no, forcing us to change our definition of a woman for Alan to a person who has a uterus, *or at any time has had one.*)

Eventually, of course, the big moment came. I'll have to admit that I spent the better part of my twenty-one-hour labor wondering, between Lamaze breaths, how anyone with half a memory cell would — outside of gross and unforgivable carelessness — willfully and with forethought ever choose to go through this process a second time. But moments after Henri was born (with benefit of spinal anesthesia), I was ready to have eight more children just so I could go through the birth process again and again.

It's funny. I used to think childbirth was the price you paid to get the kid. Now it seems like the kid is the price you pay for getting to go through childbirth.

Ralph, by the way, was absolutely wonderful throughout the delivery. He breathed with me, encouraged me, and did not eat his hot-pastrami sandwich in front of me. There is little more you can ask of a husband.

Frankly, it sounds a little odd to explain to people that the peak experience of your life occurred under anesthesia. (I went into labor fully intending not to have any, but around the eighteenth hour, the reasons suddenly eluded me.) Actually, it was partly because of the spinal (epidural) that it *was* such a wonderful experience. I was alert, relaxed, and able to take in the whole show.

The reason I bring this up is that I realize it is now practically un-American to have pain relief during childbirth. And I'll be the first to agree that there are highly compelling arguments against anesthesia, bottle feeding, and hospital deliveries. There are, however, sometimes highly compelling reasons for them too. (I remember a woman in our Lamaze class asking with unbridled hostility after a talk on anesthesia, "Doctor, has anyone ever *died* of pain?" "No," he replied, "but I've known some women in labor who wished they would.")

The first three days after Henri's birth, I was floating on a cloud of euphoria. This was actually quite convenient, because in point of fact I could not walk or sit. I'll never laugh at anyone with hemorrhoids again.

Frankly, this was the one part of childbirth I was totally unprepared for. Many friends had alluded to "sore bottoms," a euphemism, as it turns out, only slightly less tragic than "fussy" babies. (You offer the baby the world, your basal ganglia in the palm of your hand, so he'll stop crying, only to have your pediatrician remark, "Oh, he's just being a little fussy." You can't believe you're talking about the same kid.)

My obstetrician, of course, quite reasonably pointed out that one should expect some discomfort when the episiotomy is almost as long as the baby. (Henri, I should mention, was enormous.) All I know is that by the third postpartum day, I had a desperate case of Terminal Tush.

Now, this is one of those ailments that even those graphic childbirth books never really confront. Partly, I suppose, it is because no one actually dies of it, and because it does eventually clear up, usually just about the time you're making serious inquiries into perineal transplants. In the meantime, however, it is a foregone conclusion that your sex life is ruined, you'll never leave the house again without your doughnut-shaped pillow, and that your intestinal tract is in rigor mortis. At the height of these concerns, the hospital sends you home.

The postpartum experience (or, What's a nice person like me doing in a place like this?)

The first day home, 11:00 A.M.: Ralph and Alan came to the hospital this morning to bring Henri and me home. I was feeling somewhat reluctant about this as it still takes me upward of four minutes to lower myself into a seat, and of course, it goes without saying that I'll never walk right again. How in this condition can I possibly keep up with a two-year-old, particularly one who delights in such semisuicidal activities as swan dives off the top of the refrigerator? Ralph, however, was desperate to have me home, maintaining that he could not vouch for Alan's safety if he had to spend another whole day with him.

Ralph and Alan had hung a big *"Welcome Home"* sign on the front porch and were so pleased at my reaction. Alan ran into the house to get some toys to show his new brother. "Look, Henri, see?" (He shoves the toy right in Henri's face.) Henri screams. Ralph yells at Alan. "I just want show Henri my truck!" sobs Alan defensively. It is a sobering realization that I have just witnessed a scenario that will be played out again and again for the next . . . *eighteen years?*

2:00 P.M.: Our favorite grandmotherly babysitter, Freida, mercifully arrives to help me while Ralph goes off to the office for a few hours. After four days of babysitting, I have never seen Ralph so anxious to go to work. I am a captive of my rocking chair. Henri lies in one arm, alternately sleeping and eating, Alan nestles in the other, overcome with curiosity about Henri's tiny little parts. Finally he tires of this and inquires when Henri will be going back to the hospital.

5:00 P.M.: In an effort to be helpful, Freida has spent the afternoon folding the laundry and cleaning my refrigerator. Anxious to do things right, she consults with me about the placement of each item in the refrigerator and the proper place to put each item of clothing. I tell her "anywhere," but she is undeterred. Despite efforts to divert him with *Sesame Street* (blaring in the background), Alan has as many questions about the baby as Freida does about the laundry. I want to make this day easier for Alan, but I don't have the energy. Henri is howling. Alan is hungry. Over the din, I ask Freida if she would take the chicken on the kitchen counter out of the package and stick it in the oven. A few seconds later, she is back.

FREIDA   The whole package?

LOUISE   Yes, thank you. The whole package, if you would.

FREIDA   *(Thirty seconds later, holding up two pans)* Which one of these should I use?

LOUISE   Oh, either one.

FREIDA   *(Twenty seconds later, chicken breast in hand)* Do you trim off this fat here?

LOUISE   Any way you want to do it. Really, you don't have to trim it at all as far as I'm concerned.

FREIDA   *(Forty-five seconds later, a thigh in hand)* Now, this I'm *sure* you'll want me to trim.

LOUISE   *(trying to feed Henry with Alan hanging from her neck)* Really, Freida, don't feel you have to — cut it out, Alan — go to any special trouble. We're trying to make things — didn't Mommy *just tell you?* — very simple tonight so all you have to do is — get your foot out of Henri's face — put the chicken in the pan and stick it in the — I'll make your supper in just a minute — oven — no, he *doesn't* like that and I can't breathe either — at three-fifty. OK?

FREIDA   *(Twenty seconds later)* Of course, you'll want me to wash it.

LOUISE   No wash. No salt. Just oven.

FREIDA   *(Forty seconds later)* I don't understand this oven. No, don't get up! I'll figure it out. *(Five minutes later)* Don't be alarmed about the gas smell, I opened the windows. I forgot to ask, breast side up or breast side down?

LOUISE   *(tears starting to well up in her eyes from fatigue, gas fumes, and Alan standing on her crotch)* Um, up.

FREIDA   I always cook mine down.

LOUISE   *(tears streaming down her cheeks)* OK, down.

FREIDA   But then again, it's your house . . .

LOUISE   *(sobbing uncontrollably)* I DON'T CARE! PLEASE! JUST PUT THE CHICKEN IN THE PAN AND PUT IT IN THE OVEN!

FREIDA   There, there, dear. The first day home is always the worst.

Day 6:   I'm not even minding night feedings this time as it's my only chance to be alone with the baby. I can't seem to get enough of him, examining his little body, rocking him, holding him.

The phone rang this morning while I was feeding Henri, and before I could get it, Alan answered. "Hi, this is Alan," he announced brightly. "I have a new baby brother, Henri. My mommy has a sick tush!" Well, it's one way to get rid of magazine salesmen.

Day 9:   Alan looks at me so mournfully at times. I am grieving too that things for the two of us will never be the same again.

Congratulations card arrived today from Ralph's mother, spelling my name wrong.

Day 12:   Things seem to be getting into some kind of routine here. Either that or we are simply getting used to chaos. I decided last week that my standards will simply have to relax a little for the next few months or I will go crazy.

Day 14:   Ralph and I and the pillow went out for dinner. Freida kindly babysat. Not to worry, she said, but she didn't sit comfortably for three years.

Day 17:   Alan never wants to eat until I sit down to feed Henri. Then terminal starvation sets in. "I huuuuuuungry, Mommy!" he wails, with piteous, imploring eyes as he clings to my leg. Ten minutes earlier he had refused all offers of sustenance. I tell him he will have to wait a few minutes. "No, NOW. I need eat NOW," he sobs, collapsing on the floor at the foot of the rocker. Sometimes I think God put children on this earth to show parents how good they had it before.

Day 20:   Even in this short time, Alan has become more independent, taking himself to the potty, helping fetch things for me. People keep telling me that it's good to have a sibling so they'll learn to share. Try looking into the eyes of a two-year-old and telling *him* that.

Day 24:   I am going crazy. House is filthy. Ralph and Alan seem to be constitutionally incapable of picking up anything. I seem to be constitutionally incapable of letting them get away with it. Ralph said, get a cleaning lady. I said, we already have one.

Day 29:   Henri is fortunately possessed of a delightful disposition. I am struck by how different his reality will be from Alan's. Even at four weeks, Henri knows that the world is a dangerous place, inhabited by predatory older brothers who can't resist testing just how strongly he is glued together. Already Henri has four distinct cries: hunger, wetness, fatigue, and "get that blond kid away from me." Alan can actually be quite gentle with the baby, imitating me as he soothes and caresses him. Lately, however, he has taken to heart-stopping pronouncements. "Mommy, I teach baby Henri eat a bagel!" Or, appearing with watering can in hand, "I pretend baby Henri is a flower!" You have to have a strong constitution to be a mommy.

Day 35:   I was giving Henri his 11:00 P.M. feeding when Ralph wandered in all distressed-looking and announced that frankly, our sex life has been terrible lately. I burst out laughing. Then I realized he was serious.

Day 40:   One morning a week, Ralph takes both kids so I can have some time to myself. It's funny. I used to hate being alone in the house. Now I can't wait. Sometimes life events are very therapeutic.

Day 45:   Alan alternates between being an utter delight and just awful. The other afternoon, I was taking a nap; Alan tiptoed in, laid a handful of slightly mangled daisies on my pillow, and whispered in my ear, "I love you, Mommy." (I forgave him everything, past and future.) Yesterday, however, he was harassing the baby all morning. After I scolded him for the third time, he looked me in the eye and said, "I don't think Henri likes you, Mommy."

Day 49: I think Ralph is suffering from postpartum depression. Lately he has become very demanding and grouchy, maintaining that "nobody" seems to have time for him anymore. I tried to convey to him that "nobody" is overwhelmed herself.

Day 54: We planned a family outing this morning to the park, but black storm clouds were lurking overhead when we got up and I thought we should cancel. But Ralph was adamant and he and Alan finally set off in the car in the midst of a torrential downpour. So poor was the visibility that they were promptly in a minor traffic accident — Ralph's very first. The damage was probably more to Ralph's ego than the car, as evidenced by his call to our insurance company. "This is Ralph DeGrave," he reported tersely, "and I'd like to report a scratch."

Day 60: In spite of night feedings, sibling rivalry, and perineal paralysis, this has been the happiest two months of my life. (Ralph says I could have fooled him.)

Day 71: Alan DeGrave on the seventy-first day of his brother's life: "I hope baby Henri get smished!" I think Ralph and I make the mistake of thinking that if you talk to a kid about his hostile feelings, he won't have them anymore. Actually, all you have is an openly hostile kid.

Day 85: Henri was in his Jolly Jumper this morning (one of those harnesses connected to a spring that attaches to a doorframe), happily bouncing his little heart out. I left him alone for just a second to put the wash into the dryer, only to overhear Alan cheerfully announce, "Here you go, baby Henri!" I dropped the clothes and rushed back, just as

Henri shot by. It is beginning to amaze me that so many baby brothers survive to adulthood.

Day 90: There is a lot to be said for not letting them outnumber you. That is to say, it's a lot easier to be with the kids separately than together. Tuesdays when Alan goes to nursery school, I spend the entire morning blissfully rocking Henri for two uninterrupted hours, chores be damned. Thursdays, Alan and I spend the afternoon alone, and it's like the old days. Alan seems to be slowly adapting to this massive jolt on his Richter scale, though he is the first to admit that life for him was better before. I hope someday that Alan and Henri will share the same closeness that Marie and I have, however unlikely it seems at the moment. Henri slept through the night for the first time two days ago; it would be an understatement to say that this is a major improvement in my life. Ralph is suddenly a lot more cheerful again; he has stopped wandering around muttering, "Who needs me? I only support this operation." Slowly we seem to have made the transition from three to four.

Very slowly.

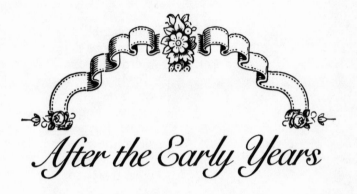

After the Early Years

After the first few years of marriage, the partners may experience a need to reevaluate the basis on which they initially came together. Questions of fidelity, appreciation, family ties, and roles in the marriage are brought into focus. Key issues at this stage are endless in their variety—from clarification of values and choosing a style of living satisfactory to both, to concern over a decrease in the physical prowess of youth. The career that one partner worked so many years to attain may suddenly seem routine and boring. Annoying habits in the spouse that once seemed at least tolerable no longer seem so.

On the other hand, the resolution of these issues may promote in the couple a new and more sustaining level of friendship.

This is not a speedy process.

The big reward

It was a momentous day for us when, nine years after we met and seven years after we were married, Ralph finally had both graduate school and the Navy behind him, and was able to open his own office. There had been plenty of sacrifice on both our parts, and we had looked forward to this day for a long, long time.

Several weeks after Ralph was officially open for business, I picked him up after work and we decided to stop at our favorite ice-cream parlor on the way home.

"Hi, Ralph. Hi, Louise," said our waitress. "Don't tell me — one hot-fudge sundae with vanilla, one dish of butter pecan, and bring the hot fudge on the side so you can split it, right?"

(It's almost frightening when people know you that well.)

"No," said Ralph, "we are entering a new era in our lives. We will have two hot-fudge sundaes."

Then we went across the street to the nearest department store and bought Ralph his first full-price, nonirregular shirt.

"Maybe this is premature," I said anxiously to Ralph, who was counting out $12.00 in nickles, dimes, and quarters for the sales clerk. (Business wasn't exactly booming yet.)

Then we went home for a steak dinner, a bottle of wine, and an acute depressive reaction.

"This is going to sound absurd," said Ralph, "but what is there to live for when you can buy two hot-fudge sundaes outright?"

"You know," I said, "that's exactly what I was thinking."

We were silent for a moment, reminiscing.

"Remember when you graduated from school," I said, "and we traded in Aunt Mara's Cross pen for a top sheet?"

Ralph brightened immediately. "Remember how we used to get my shirts at that outlet store on the Lower East Side that sold irregulars? The ones where the buttonholes never matched up to the button and you had to make sure they had two sleeves?"

"Yes, but they were great bargains," I recalled. "Remember how we'd go to Chinatown afterward and get pork fried rice and drink tea out of hospital glasses at that really cheap place where you got food poisoning?"

"Those were the days," said Ralph wistfully. "You know, I wish I hadn't bought that shirt. I thought it was going to make me so happy."

"We could always return it," I said tentatively. "Real stores let you return things."

"All these years I've been working toward this day, to be out of school, to be through with the Navy, to open up my own office. The Big Reward."

"Well, I guess this is the Big Reward," I said. "Feel any different?"

"No," said Ralph. "You?"

"No," I said.

We were silent for a while.

"I guess I never really realized it before," said Ralph finally.

"Realized what?" I said.

Ralph smiled wryly. "That the Big Reward was all along."

Ends of eras

The fall of our seventh anniversary was the end of an era for us. Ralph retired from his music career.

For some reason, I found myself feeling all emotional about it, even though I had sometimes had considerable ambivalence about Ralph being a musician. It wasn't exactly a social boon to be engaged to a man who worked Friday and Saturday evenings, twenty-five consecutive nights during the Christmas season, and every New Year's Eve.

When I first met Ralph he was putting himself through college and graduate school playing piano and organ in a band. People often ask me what kind of band. I guess the best answer to that is whatever kind you needed that night, *that* kind of band.

Since I only saw Ralph on weekends anyway, our entire courtship was conducted during band breaks. I don't even think we danced together until our third anniversary. Every time we went to a place where there was music, Ralph was playing it.

I used to go to all the jobs during the first few years of our marriage when we were young and in love, but by the sixth year, I had learned to be more selective. For example, never go to a banquet job. There you are sitting politely on your folding chair in the corner salivating into your lap while the waiters wheel a seven-course dinner by you. (And Cinderella thought *she* had it tough.)

I guess the basic reason I stopped going all the time, though, was that it was just too hard on my ego. Face it, there is no lower form of animal life than the piano player's wife at a gig. You'd be sitting there trying to act invisible and some well-meaning guest would come gushing over and say, "Oh, Harold, look at this darling little girl sitting all by herself in the corner! Let's introduce her to Malcolm. Don't you know anyone here, dear?"

"Actually, no. I'm a friend of the band."

"Oh, I didn't realize." (To Harold.) "Just some hussy with the band."

I still like to think I was an asset to Ralph's whole operation. Even if the management had occasional qualms about me, the sax man, bass player, and drummer did not. I think this was because of my sunny good nature and because it was not lost on any of them, as I staggered from car to stage with their equipment, that one should not look a packhorse in the mouth. Ralph used to say he married me because I could dismantle a Hammond organ and load it into a truck.

I don't want to give the impression I didn't have fun. There were definite advantages. Since the band rehearsed at our house, I was the only woman on the block who hung out her laundry accompanied by a live, four-piece group.

I think what I liked best about band jobs was that I got a chance to see groups of people I would normally never come in contact with. Ralph played the highs and lows, from exclusive clubs to some of those organizations who aptly named themselves after animals.

Sometimes the band acted as a kind of buffer, like at a tense social gathering where the guests didn't like each other. Frequently Ralph would send me to check things out while the group was setting up. "I don't know, Ralph," I'd report back. "The bride's family is wearing military uniforms and the groom's are in turbans. I'd play really loud if I were you."

The fall of our seventh year, however, Ralph said that now that he had graduated from school and had a "real" career, he had less time and didn't need the money so desperately anymore.

So that year, there would be no more coat pockets full of spare bow ties. No Ralph leaping into the car after work and barreling down the highway at eighty miles an hour, simultaneously changing into a tux. No accidentally dropping the organ into a snowbank. No watching the band fall apart when the dancer turned out to be a stripper. No frantically flipping through fake books for the music to "Moon over Tuscaloosa," the guest of honor's favorite song. No blowing my little horn from my folding chair in the corner at the stroke of twelve on New Year's Eve.

Looked like a dim Christmas.

Marriage: Open, closed, or slightly ajar

I can't begin to describe what a shock it was the morning Ralph and I woke up and realized we had a closed marriage.

"We are so symbiotic that I almost can't tell where I leave off and you begin," I said to Ralph.

This realization came after we'd had an argument the night before. It was the same old argument, but it took us an hour to realize that we were each using the other person's customary lines.

"Do you realize," I said later, "that we no longer see a movie if both of us don't want to see it? We don't see couples if one of us doesn't like one of them. Neither of us has any individual friends anymore."

If we were this close after seven years of marriage, by our twelfth anniversary, if one of us died, the other would have to be buried with him.

"Maybe we should do more things separately," said Ralph.

"How separately, how much, and with whom?" I said. I

thought it was a good idea, but that the limits needed to be defined.

We talked about many alternatives, including what is commonly referred to as "open marriage."

"I don't know," said Ralph. "From our experience with our friends, it always seems that open marriage is the official step you take before legal separation. It's like trying to turn a lemon into lemonade before you realize that even the lemon is rotten."

"My main problem with open marriage is that I don't think I could stay home maturely and unpossessively reading a socially relevant novel while you were out being 'open' with the greater metropolitan area," I said. "Unless, of course, I was the one who was out and you were home with the book." The idea began to sound increasingly appealing.

"Women in this society have to be careful of their reputations," cautioned Ralph, no doubt thinking of him out and me home with the book.

After talking about it for a few days, we did decide that it might be a good idea for us at least to take some separate classes. "Because right now," said Ralph, "we are in the position of having merged into a single being with virtually no differentiation of our separate identities."

"C'mon, it's not *that* bad," I said, but the next day I registered for a photography class.

"Last name, please," said the lady at the registration desk.

"DeGrave," I said.

"First name?"

"Mrs."

The double standard strikes again

I always love reading in magazines about all those liberated couples who share household chores. But there is one question those articles never answer: By whose standards do you do them?

This has always been a real problem around our house. I don't have that much trouble getting Ralph to do dishes. The problem I have is getting him to do them in such a way that I don't have to do them over again afterward.

From outward appearances, Ralph and I seem to have virtually identical standards. When we first decided to divide up the chores, we both agreed wholeheartedly that the end result should conform to the basic standard of cleanliness. The problem is, we have never agreed since what cleanliness is.

I remember peering over Ralph's shoulder one night about three years ago just as he was finishing the dinner dishes. "Ralph," I said, "I don't want to seem critical, but about that pan . . ."

"What's wrong with it?" said Ralph.

"Well," I said, "there's still food in it."

"Where?" said Ralph defensively. I showed him. "A little ring of tomato sauce around the rim," said Ralph, clearly annoyed. "I'd hardly call that 'food.'"

Now, the writers of those magazine articles might have suggested resolving that particular situation by assigning Ralph the tasks that he likes, and would, if life were logical, do well. The problem I have with that is that if these are supposed to be liberated relationships, how come the guy is always getting dibsies on all the good chores? It is a safe bet that if given a choice, he isn't going to choose cleaning the toilet.

The question of whose standards should prevail got even harder on less well-defined tasks — like writing thank-you notes, for example. We had received a lot of nice baby gifts for our kids, and to make the job of writing the notes go faster, we had decided to divide up the list and each take half.

Well, one of the gifts we received was a baby book that had specific spaces for you to record every detail you can imagine about the baby's first few years of life. Or almost every detail, anyway.

"Dear Sam and Janice," I read surreptitiously over Ralph's shoulder. "Thank you for the baby book. You must have diagnosed Louise's compulsiveness well since she has already filled in most of the spaces. I think I should point out, however, that there is no page for size and consistency of bowel movements, nor —"

"Ralph," I said, "you can't write that!"

"What's wrong with it?" said Ralph. "I like it. Look, if I'm going to write thank-you notes, I reserve the right to do them my way." He glanced at the next item on our list. "Hmmmm, drool bibs. You know, this is more fun than I expected."

An hour later, we each had a tidy pile of notes stacked up next to us.

"Want to read any of mine before I seal them up?" offered Ralph.

"Thanks, but no," I said stoically. Ralph looked up, genuinely surprised. "I think, Ralph," I continued, "I have found the solution to our problem."

"What's that?" said Ralph.

"To stop," I sighed resignedly, "looking over your shoulder."

I never thought I'd hear myself say this, but sometimes it's easier not to know.

Life with His Highness

Now that he was earning a little money for the first time in his life, Ralph was acting like an Arab oil sheik.

"Ralph," I told him one morning, "it's your week to do the grocery shopping."

"It's not worth my time anymore," said Ralph. "Why don't we hire somebody?"

I had to say in all honesty that, nine years before, I never would have envisioned our having this discussion. Whenever it came down to a question of whether it was worth our time to save a little money, you better believe it was. I drove all the way across town to save a grand total of twenty-five cents on chickens. (The gas probably cost me forty cents.)

"Ah, the problems of the idle rich," I said to Ralph. "What you are neglecting to consider is that I earn at a rate of only six dollars per hour."

"I never thought of it that way," said Ralph. "You're perfectly right. It is definitely worth your time to go grocery shopping."

As Ralph saw it, there was no point in doing anything he didn't want to anymore when there was probably some individual lurking around willing to perform a reasonable facsimile of the task at a fraction of Ralph's hourly salary. (His business had started to do well.)

"Well, Ralph," I said, "while we're hiring out your domestic chores, why don't we hire someone to *live* for you too?"

> WANTED: *Masochistic individual to take over seamy side of up-and-coming young man's life. Must be willing to perform all manner of household drudgery, including shopping, dishwashing, and changing the dial on the TV set. Must also be willing to endure occasional insomnia, tennis elbow, several strains of flu, and to feel a full range of negative feelings, including depression, anxiety, anger, and constipation.*

As Ralph's earning power increased, he found more and more items affordable that had previously been out of our price range, and naturally he began buying them. At the same time, I increasingly began wondering why I was going to work. On a good day, Ralph made more in eight hours than I made in ten days.

In most ways, I was delighted. We'd had enough years of struggling. And heaven knew Ralph deserved to see the fruits of so many years of labor.

And, of course, our situation could certainly be used to my advantage. If, for example, I saw a sporty little outfit that I would have previously rejected as too expensive, I could say to myself, "Now, is this worth two short hours of Ralph's time? Of course it is."

The basic issue, I think, was that I was no longer feeling useful. Always before we were a team; we *needed* my income, however modest.

One afternoon we were standing outside the bike shop looking at ten-speed bikes through the window. Ralph had never in his life had a new bike of any speed and had always thought what a luxury it would be to just walk into a store and buy a bike. At the time he had a three-speed used one.

"I think," said Ralph, "I'm going to get one."

Always before, we'd tended to think in terms of relative values. For example, given a quarter, you could have a German Chocolate Cake ice-cream cone, or fifteen seconds of psychoanalysis. This always helped put purchases in perspective.

"I don't know, Ralph," I said. "Is this bike worth fifty-two trips to the zoo? Three visits to the infertility clinic?"

"You betcha," said Ralph.

"Forty hours of my time before taxes?"

"Oh, consider it my treat," said Ralph graciously.

I can't quite explain it, but I had this sudden feeling I'd just become obsolete.

Protecting the spouse from worry

Ralph used to say his biggest problem was that people were always trying to protect him from worry.

Take his parents, for example. Since we lived so far away, Ralph would call them every Sunday to find out how they were doing. Well, in one week their dog got run over; Aunt Ada broke her hip; and Uncle Hermie, visiting from New York, dropped dead of a heart attack in their living room.

So Ralph, unaware of any of these events, calls and says, "How's everything?"

"So-so," says Ralph's father. "A little rainy perhaps."

To be honest, I was as bad as Ralph's parents sometimes, though I think I would have managed to mention it to Ralph if a close relative had died in our living room.

Now, this may seem in direct contradiction to what I said before—that Ralph didn't worry *enough*. And it's true, I definitely felt Ralph could have worried a little more about some of the mechanics of our daily living. But there is worry and there is *worry*—a fundamental, pervasive, lose-sleep-over-it, brooding concern. I couldn't bear that Ralph should suffer the latter on my behalf.

Once, I remember, when I was trying to cultivate a freelance writing career, I got four stories back with rejection slips in one day. I was despondent. But I just couldn't bear to tell Ralph; he would have been so hurt for me.

"How was your day, honey?" said Ralph when he came home.

"Oh, just great!" I said, a model of composure. Then I burst into tears. I may have been better at dead relatives, but Ralph's parents were better stoics.

This need that the folks and I had to protect Ralph from worry drove Ralph absolutely crazy.

"What is it about me that everybody wants to do my worrying for me?" said Ralph exasperatedly when he learned his parents had kept the news of Uncle Hermie from him. "I feel like a magnet for martyrs."

"Your parents know the pressures you're under," I suggested. "They don't want to burden you with their problems."

"But it's been that way all my life!" said Ralph. "It was like a state secret when my cousin Sidney had shock treatments."

"They probably felt it would be too traumatic for a child who wasn't old enough to understand," I said.

"I was twenty-two," said Ralph, "and I hardly knew my cousin Sidney. That's just it. It may have been OK when I was a child, but now I am an adult. And bad enough that my parents still persist in protecting me, but now you're starting up too!"

"I'm just afraid you'll worry," I said.

"Perhaps," said Ralph, "but not nearly as much as I worry wondering what you're not telling me because I'll worry."

"Well," I said tentatively, "I didn't want to upset you, but all of my last four stories came back with rejection slips, that torn cartilage in my knee just keeps getting worse and worse, and the Vega is now burning a quart of oil per week."

"I'm really sorry to hear all that," said Ralph compassionately. "See? I didn't disintegrate."

A few hours later, though, I caught him staring off into space, occasionally mumbling to himself. Even though he said he'd prefer to know, it hurt me to see that he was worried about me. I moved closer to see if I could hear what he was saying.

Ralph shifted slightly in his chair, shaking his head sadly. "A quart of oil per week," he sighed.

Who's getting all the giving

In the six years that I've lived in California, I have frequently heard people say, "From now on, I'm going to stop spending so much time taking care of other people and start taking care of *me.*"

In the six years that I've lived in California, however, I have never heard anyone say, "Wow, I can't believe how people are always knocking themselves out to meet my needs."

So what I want to know is, who's getting all the goodies? If everyone feels like he's giving and nobody's admitting to getting, where's all that giving going?

"Beats me," said Ralph when I asked him one night.

"Maybe people just have difficulty realizing how much other people really do for them," I suggested. "For example, I sometimes feel you have no idea how much I do for you."

"Since you mention it," said Ralph, "I sometimes feel you have no idea how much I do for you either."

"Yes," I said, "but my whole *life* revolves around your life."

"But," said Ralph, "my whole life revolves around your life too."

"Are we talking about the same two lives?" I said.

"Maybe we really *don't* realize how much we get from each other," said Ralph.

"Just as an example," I said, "what's the last thing you did for me?"

"Well," said Ralph, "I came home last night."

"You were thinking of going somewhere else?"

"I had a really hard day yesterday," said Ralph, "and as I was leaving my office, I had this sudden impulse to just get in the car and go drive around for a while, maybe stop someplace if I felt like it and listen to some music."

"And you didn't feel you could do that?"

"I knew you and Alan were looking forward to my coming home, and you'd have dinner already made and all. Now, for argument's sake, what's the last thing you did for me?"

"I was home waiting with dinner ready."

"You were thinking of going someplace else?"

"Well, no," I said. "It's just that the only reason I cook is for you. Left to my own devices, I'd live off salads."

"I guess I always take your cooking for granted," said Ralph. "I hate salads."

"Since you mention it," I said, "I'll admit I do tend to take your coming home for granted too. I really enjoy your companionship."

"I think," said Ralph, "maybe we just answered the question about what happens to all that giving."

"Yeah," I said. "I guess it gets lost in the woods."

Old husband, new dimensions

Just when you think you know a person well, you come across a whole new dimension of his personality.

For example, Ralph has always insisted that not only was he totally lacking in writing ability, but that the writing process was so torturous for him that it was only under extreme duress that he was able to set more than four consecutive words to paper. It was for this reason that I had always been relegated to conducting all written communications during our marriage.

It was during our eighth year, however, that Ralph's mother supplied me with evidence that not only did Ralph possess considerable literary potential but that at least once in his life he had been sufficiently motivated to use it.

The evidence was Ralph's eighth-grade yearbook.

"Ralph's hobbies are playing the piano and the trombone," said the inscription next to his picture. "He likes baseball best of all sports. Ralph is president of the Student Council. He has an ability to do everything. He also has a nice personality and is well liked."

It was a glowing portrait of a talented and popular twelve-year-old Ralph . . . which just happens to have been written by Ralph himself.

As the editor of the yearbook, Ralph wrote all the inscriptions, including his own. (It's amazing the lengths some kids will go to ensure a favorable image for posterity.)

Actually, as I read over the annual, it was clear to me why Ralph was chosen for the job. The kid clearly had an unusual talent for the brief characterization and for capturing the essence of early adolescence:

"Bob is interested in sports. His hobby is model airplanes. His favorite saying is 'Beans.' He wants to be a Fuller-Brush Man . . ."

"Dorrie has a very nice personality and gets along with everyone. Her hobby is collecting miniature china cocker spaniels and matchbook covers. Her favorite saying is 'Shut up' . . ."

"Harvey served on the Newspaper Club from September to April but then because of graduation exercises he thought it best to resign. His hobby is playing intellectual games. His pet peeve is waves that don't break."

"Fred is a member of the Refreshments Committee. He is also interested in girls. He wants to go to Princeton University and become a millionaire lawyer."

"Gregory is shy and quiet and gets along well with everyone. He is seen most with his cat . . ."

"Christine is a member of the Newspaper Club and is friendly with everyone. She is interested in typing. Her favorite expression is 'Oh gosh.' "

"John's ambition lies in the field of medicine. He plans to go to high school next year . . ."

"Eddie's hobby is girls as is his interest. His ambition is to be a truck driver. His favorite song is the Hawaiian War Chant."

"Sandy is a great animal lover although she has no pets at the present. She also collects baseball cards . . ."

"Allen's ambition is to be an orthodontist when he grows up. His favorite saying is Oh! He is in Conservation Club and enjoys collecting pin-ups . . ."

That was the day Ralph had his last letter written for him.

If it's not one thing, it's another

One day not long before our ninth anniversary, Ralph came home and announced he wanted to get a goldfish in a large glass bowl and hang it in a macrame hanger like he'd seen at someone else's home.

"It sounds very attractive," I admitted.

"So we'll get one?" said Ralph.

"Absolutely not."

"What do you mean, 'absolutely not'? I thought you just said you liked the idea."

"I do. But I will not maintain one more thing in this house."

"What's to maintain? You throw a little food in every other day. It'll take three minutes a week."

"Three minutes a week?" I really thought I was going to be hysterical.

"What's so funny?" said Ralph.

"Ralph," I said, "we said that about each of our twenty-two current houseplants, six citrus trees, two avocado plants, the dog, the checking account, five major appliances, six minor appliances, two cars, and the stereo. And you know what, Ralph? We were right. It *does* take only three minutes a week for most of those things. Under normal circumstances."

Here's where I started to get *really* hysterical.

"The problem is, Ralph, we have not had a normal week in nine years! Under 'normal' circumstances, the fruit trees do not have woolly whitefly, the ferns do not have scale, the spider plants don't need repotting, the geraniums aren't being devoured by snails, a dining-room chair isn't broken, the car isn't hit and run, the shower drain drains, the self-clean is cleaning, the seat-belt buzzer only buzzes when it's supposed to, the dryer doesn't break a gasket, the dog doesn't develop an allergic reaction to his DHL shot, the washing machine isn't making funny noises, the baby doesn't get an ear infection, the record changer changes records, and the checkbook isn't overdrawn! And that was only *last* month.

"You may not believe this, Ralph, but every single thing we own seems to develop pressing personal problems. And now you want to stick me with a goldfish!" I started sobbing uncontrollably. "I can't stand it!"

"Gee, I'm sorry I mentioned it," said Ralph apologetically.

"What happens when the goldfish develops asthma and needs special medications?" I cried. "What happens when its bowl gets algae? When its marbles get dirty? When it develops an allergy to domestic dead flies and requires a special formulation of imported ones available only in a pet store in Los Angeles? Who will arrange for its welfare when we go on vacation? Who will replace its macrame hanger when it starts to rot? Who will replace the fish itself when it croaks?"

For a long moment neither of us spoke.

"Ralph," I sighed, "I wasn't meant to be a home manager. I was meant to live in a predecorated, one-bedroom apartment around the corner from a laundromat."

"A little one-bedroom apartment," echoed Ralph, "with space for your darkroom, a yard for the baby, a ten-by-fifteen 'alcove' for you to work in, a — "

"Precisely," I said.

Confessions of a college-athlete-turned-klutz

Having a desk job, I began to feel I wasn't getting enough exercise. So one summer, I signed up for a daily volleyball class at the beach.

Actually, I picked volleyball because I had such fond memories of informal games in college. I remember how I always tried to be on Myra ("The Gorilla") Galinski's team, first because I liked winning and second because nothing before or since has ever struck fear in my heart as the sight of Myra, airborne, summoning all the archetypal strength of her anthropoid ancestors, as she smashed a spike shot at my head with a bloodcurdling "Gunga Din!"

"The first thing," said the instructor at the introductory session of my class at the beach, "is that we cannot play volleyball unless we are in shape." No problem, I'd always been in shape.

For the next fifteen minutes, we made like the Marine Corps — one, two, up, down, side, side, *move.* I didn't do as well on the exercises as I would have liked.

"OK," said the instructor, "now we're going to sprint down to the jetty and back. Hey, you lying facedown in the sand, let's go."

When I got to the jetty, I noted that the rest of the class was already back at the court while I was ready to drop dead. (A most embarrassing predicament.) So what do you do if you're a good obsessive-compulsive from an achievement-oriented family about to have a coronary but not about to admit it, while your coach and classmates are yelling, "C'mon, Louise, *faster!*"

Well, you could just quietly jog behind the bathhouse, then when they've forgotten about you, stagger to your car and slip away. But no, Dad always said you have to finish the race.

(Dad, of course, paid dearly for instilling that bit of character. When my sister Marie and I sailed in sailboat races as kids—not our idea at all, by the way—he would always be standing on the shore waiting for us to come in, about four hours after everyone else had finished, been awarded prizes, had an extended picnic, and gone home.)

Or, I could pretend I sprained my ankle and that's what was holding me up. (Once, in eighth grade, I brought up the rear of a track competition announcing brightly, "Not bad for someone just recovering from polio," so the sprained-ankle idea was actually a huge developmental step.)

Well, back at the court (with my sprained ankle), we did an hour of strenuous, competitive serving exercises, the losers (guess who?) having to do pushups, followed by a couple of running relays and another race to the jetty. (My ankle flared up again, so I sat that one out.)

I guess what really disturbed me about my new role as the class klutz was that several years before, in my youth, I had been an adequate athlete. I'd always been an avid walker and swimmer. In high school I'd played on intramural hockey and soccer teams. In college I'd played squash and volleyball. I'd even been pretty good at fencing. I couldn't figure out how it had happened, but in the six years of desk jobs since I'd graduated from college, my coordination just sort of wandered away when I wasn't looking.

For the first few days of my volleyball class, I kept thinking I wasn't really out of shape generally but just unpracticed in certain areas of fine motor coordination. (This is known in psychiatric circles as "denial.") That was until I got paired up with a fifteen-year-old girl in class whose only comment to me all week was, "Boy, Louise, are you a spaz!"

I was crushed and unbelieving.

"Ralph," I said to my husband when I got home that night, "a punk called me a spaz."

"It shouldn't take you too long to get back into shape," said Ralph, who was in terrific shape.

Frankly, I still think I wasn't all that out of shape; I just looked that way compared to the competition. My rotten luck, I ended up in a class full of lithe, athletic, suntanned college girls with little upturned noses and devastating coordination, who wiggled and giggled a lot and who all seemed to be named Cathy.

I probably would have left right there if it hadn't been for the coach, who had a warm heart, the patience of a saint, an unlimited supply of encouragement, and I think a Ph.D. in athletic supporters. He also seemed to be on intimate terms with most of the Cathys.

I quickly realized that if I didn't shape up in this class, it wouldn't be because the coach didn't try.

"I want you to *explode* out of the sand, leap into the air, and smash that ball over the net," he said. "Let's practice. One, two, three, *explode! explode!*"

Nothing gets you into shape like exploding, let me tell you. But after an hour, the only things that were exploding were my internal organs.

"Louise," he said, "you're not exploding."

"Would you settle for a small incendiary blaze?" I said.

Ralph, bless his heart, kept pointing out to me that although it's hard on the ego to be the class klutz, especially when you're not used to it (and even more especially if you are), that there were really a lot of other people out there in the same or worse condition than I who didn't have the courage to sign up for sports classes.

So come on, you cowards! Everybody out for volleyball!

Habits that drive the spouse cuckoo

I love Ralph, I really do. But if there were an Olympics for losing one's possessions, Ralph would be a gold medalist. The next day, he'd probably lose the medal.

I mean, I have long since decided that Ralph's tombstone should be engraved, "I'm sure it's around *somewhere*."

Fortunately, a lot of his stuff doesn't stay lost permanently. Most of his possessions, however, have enjoyed long periods of time during which their whereabouts were unknown.

For the first five years of our marriage, I used to wake up with Ralph whispering in my ear, "Have you seen my car keys?" When we vacationed in San Francisco, his watch stayed on another week. He has left his sunglasses on airplanes (twice) and in restaurants (122 times). His office keys, missing for some weeks on one occasion, finally turned up on page forty-six of a *Newsweek*. He has lost his appointment book so often that he now writes in the front of each new one, "When found . . ."

Because of his tendency to misplace things, Ralph's leave-taking in the morning is often a lengthy affair. The way it usually happens is that the dog and the children and I line up at the front door and we wish him a nice day and he kisses most of us good-bye. The door, however, is barely closed before he is back, wondering if I remember whether or not he brought home his briefcase last night, and if so, where it might be. Some minutes later, off he goes again, only to return before he even makes the driveway to get his wallet, which, it soon develops, he can't find.

"Ralph," I said one morning in the midst of this, "you should go into psychoanalysis and find out why you can't seem to remember where you put anything."

"That's easy," said Ralph. "I'm forgetful."

"There is no such thing as forgetful," I said. "It is a deep-seated psychological hang-up embedded in your early desire to drive your mother — and now me — crazy!"

I don't mind Ralph losing his own stuff (well, yes, I do) but he misplaces our joint property too. I remember one day I needed a screwdriver. I looked in all the usual places Ralph might have left one — in his underwear drawer, under the canned goods, holding up a floppy plant, and even, as a long shot, in the toolbox. But none of the six assorted-size screwdrivers we were rumored to own could be located.

For years I'd been threatening to buy a set of my own tools, even though it seemed a colossal waste of money. That day I did. And I hid them carefully.

Some weeks later, Ralph wandered into the kitchen.

"I can't find the Phillips screwdriver."

"Tough break," I said sympathetically.

"Could I borrow yours?"

"No."

"What do you mean, 'no'?"

"No as in 'no.' I'll never see it again."

"Oh, come on, Louise. Be reasonable."

"What do you have as collateral?"

"Look, I need it to fix the baby's walker."

A good cause, I had to admit. "Well, all right."

Fifteen minutes later, Ralph returned. "Mission accomplished," he said.

"Thanks for fixing it," I said. "And by the way, where's my screwdriver?"

A frown creased Ralph's brow. "Let's see . . . the baby was playing with it after I finished," he said. "But don't worry, it's around *somewhere.*"

What to do when your husband announces he's going into the hotel business

At first it used to really worry me when Ralph would come home announcing he was going into the hotel business.

"But Ralph, you're not serious! All those years of training! You have a nice job, a charming wife, a dog who loves you, so why are you not happy?"

Ralph, meanwhile, was sitting at the dining-room table making notes on a legal pad.

"The restaurant will feature our famous chicken cacciatore," he said. "No more than four entrees so we can maintain quality. And of course, we'll have a Latin-jazz combo on the weekends."

"We'll go away for a while, Ralph," I said. "You need a rest. Hotel business! Are you out of your skull?"

"We'll keep it a small and personal operation," said Ralph, sketching floor plans. "We'll make it health-oriented, with tennis courts and a little spa."

"It'll be a financial disaster, Ralph," I said. "Where will you ever find the capital both to finance the hotel and to pay me off for my half of our communal property?"

"Of course," said Ralph, "we'll choose a charming setting, but the food and the masseuse will be the big attractions."

Frankly, I just didn't know how to handle it. Why would an intelligent person like Ralph suddenly come up with such a cretinous idea?

Then, in a blinding flash of insight, I began to wonder: maybe I was taking him too literally. Maybe what he was really trying to say was this: "Louise, in my line of work, you feel a lot less wacko knowing you always have some alternatives, like going into the hotel business. This gives you the illusion that you are not trapped."

But there I was trying to talk him out of it, which I finally realized only made him feel *more* trapped. At breakfast he kept mentioning a recurring dream that his office building burned down and that I was hit by a truck.

So I decided to stop arguing with him about the hotel business. This in effect said, "Darling, I'll stand by you no matter what. Whither thou goest, I will go. But if you think you're wacko now, wait'll you see *me* after a month in the hotel business."

It worked. Ralph stopped talking about the hotel business. This was tantamount to saying, "Louise, I really like my current job and doubt I'll ever change it, but I needed your assurance that you'll stand by me if I do. Not that I believe you for a minute."

A few weeks later, Ralph renewed the lease on his office. And I smiled my wise-wifely smile because I'd known for some time that we weren't going into the hotel business.

But lately, I'd been thinking we might do well in antiques . . .

Money

Now that Ralph is making more money, we can fight about it on a whole new level. That's the interesting thing about money; no matter how much you have of it, you always seem to need more. It's a little like heroin, and photography equipment.

What's amazing to us is that despite a significantly higher income than when we got married, our day-to-day living doesn't seem to have changed that much. It's true that we have four sets of sheets now, get professional haircuts, don't have to run down to the bank to cover every check over $20, and live in a neighborhood where you can leave a rake out on the front lawn without someone stealing it. We even own a house, or $1,400 of one anyway. (It was a 100 percent VA loan. Great for young, first-time home buyers, but gives you a house payment like the defense budget.)

And come to think of it, we do have a Keogh retirement account, although it's only in Ralph's name. (I want my stocks back!) Actually, we asked if it could be in both our names, but the bank said no, pointing out that if Ralph dies it will automatically go to me anyway. I guess they consider death early retirement. So I suppose our standard of living has improved, even if we haven't noticed it on a day-to-day basis.

One of the issues that we've never really resolved, however, is how much money one of us can spend without the consent of the other. Obviously, neither of us begrudges the other a few clothes, on one end of the spectrum, nor would either of us buy a car without consulting the other. That, however, leaves a big gray area in between.

Now, I read an article in the newspaper that suggested that couples in our situation maintain three checking accounts —

his, hers, and theirs. In the two individual accounts, each would have a certain amount of money for which they would not be accountable to the other.

In theory I like this solution a lot. In practice, the thought of balancing not one but three fouled-up checkbooks per month excites me about as much as ironing.

Recently, I've been thinking that perhaps the reason we have been unable to resolve this problem is that the issue isn't so much one of money as of power. The reason I think this is that we rarely had this conflict prekids, when I was working full-time.

Now, nobody is more convinced of the value of motherhood than I am. Who could put a price on the services I offer, including (and especially) just being there when my children need me? Availability don't come cheap.

Recently I read an article claiming that if men had to hire out all the services mothers offered, it would cost them at least $18,000 per year. Part of me feels grossly insulted at the suggestion that you could even find help who would work that kind of hours. The other part of me just wants the $18,000.

Maybe it's society, maybe it's Ralph, maybe it's me. Probably it's all of the above. But it's hard for me to feel entitled to buy things for myself when I'm not bringing in hard, cold cash. Regardless of the inherent value of motherhood. Regardless of the fact that I've never worked so hard in my life.

Ralph, who is prone to sweeping psychological statements, maintains I haven't felt entitled since I was born. That may be true. But I felt more entitled when I was working.

Ralph, of course, insists that we're a team. What's his is mine, what's mine is his. He wouldn't dream of holding his superior earning power over me. Unless, of course, it was to his advantage in an argument.

To be fair, this has only happened twice. And afterward, Ralph apologized and swore he didn't *really* mean that I could be replaced by a $2.60-per-hour, non-English-speaking, developmentally disabled day worker. It doesn't, however, take much to fuel my anxiety.

He knows and I know that if our marriage ended through divorce or death, it wouldn't be his life-style that would change significantly, it would be mine. Even with a job, my life-style would be altered drastically, while Ralph lived financially ever after.

Ralph, naturally, doesn't see it this way at all.

"You know," he said, "I'd trade a lot of what you insist is my 'economic security' for a little of your freedom. I'd love to be able to do whatever I wanted whenever I wanted to."

"Freedom? With an infant and a two-year-old? I have news for you, Ralph. I do a lot of things I don't want to too."

"Well, at least you can do whatever you don't want to whenever you want to. And all right, I do have a superior earning power to you. But you had just as much opportunity to go to school as many years as I did. Just because you didn't do it isn't *my* fault."

"True."

"Besides which, didn't you *choose* to stay home with the kids?"

"You would rather they were raised by a babysitter?"

"You know, a lot of women would consider it a luxury to be able to stay home with their kids." (How come Ralph always knows what "a lot of women" are thinking and doing, and I don't?)

"It *is* a luxury, and I enjoy being with the kids. I'm very thankful. Until about three o'clock in the afternoon."

"I mean, if you care that much about not feeling economically dependent, you could always go out and get a job."

"If I didn't care even more about the crucial early years of my kids." (And my guilt wouldn't keep getting in the way of my ambition.)

"And you know, you may not realize it, but it puts me under tremendous financial pressure when you come up with an expensive idea. *I* have to earn the money to pay for it."

"How come it doesn't put you under tremendous financial pressure when *you* come up with an expensive idea?"

"A lot of women would love to be in your position— supported by a responsible, hardworking man who loves you. What more do you want?"

I only wish I knew.

In-laws: The fourth visit

That year during Ralph's parents' visit, Pop and I became embroiled in a discussion of women's rights.

To be honest, we never did quite get to a specific discussion of "rights." But I plan to in the future, just as soon as Pop and I resolve some fundamental philosophical differences; for example, whether or not women are human.

I think I could sum up Pop's feelings about women accurately by saying that a woman's main functions in life are to breed, serve, and keep her mouth shut.

Now, none of these are my strong points. Or weak points, depending on how you look at it. Since I am especially poor at the third, and since Pop and I were in the house together all day, this caused a certain air of tension in the household, so much so that Ralph would call home from the office twice daily to inquire anxiously, "Any fatalities yet?"

Actually, Pop and I were quite civil to one another, and even, on occasion, listened to each other. It was during one of the latter types of exchanges that Pop explained to me that when he was growing up, it would have been a terrible humiliation for a man to be seen doing the grocery shopping or serving food or changing diapers. Even the religious denomination in which he was raised had a prayer where the men thanked God each morning for not creating them women.

"Things have certainly changed," I said, tears welling up in my eyes at the thought of how bad things used to be.

"Yes, they certainly have," said Pop, tears welling up in his eyes at the thought of how much better things used to be.

Actually, I've known for a long time that Pop does not hold women's intelligence and judgment in high esteem, but for some reason it bothered me more this time than usual. I'm still trying to figure out why.

I'll admit that maybe I was a little more sensitive about it all, between not working outside the home that year and being home all day with a male son, two male dogs, and Pop — with no ally other than Mom.

Mom and I get along very well now, but after forty-two years of marriage to Pop, there was no way Mom was going to be on my side.

OK, so the ally situation was a little weak. Now, I'll also admit that I would probably have done a great deal better if I could have just ignored some of Pop's more provocative comments instead of responding to them.

"Louise," I would say to myself at breakfast, "you know that it is not true that feminists are a bunch of soreheads who are just mad because they can't get a man. So the next time Pop says that, you will simply say very calmly, 'I do not agree.' You will not argue the point further."

But then, two minutes later, Pop would refer to Gloria Steinem as "the broad with the misshapen head" and we'd be off and running.

I guess, though, when it came right down to it, what really got to me about Pop's chauvinism was that in day-to-day life, he was simply so good at it.

The second-to-last night of their visit, for example, we were all eating dinner and Pop and I were involved in this very heated discussion, and just as I'm discoursing on some finer points of feminine psychology, Pop interjects, "While you're up, Louise, would you get me the mustard?"

It was only as I was opening the refrigerator door that it occurred to me I had been sitting down.

New times

Music is so much part of Ralph's soul that when he quit the part-time piano-playing business three years ago, it wasn't long before he started talking about going into it again. (It was the next day, I think.)

For Ralph, band jobs had always been his source of livelihood throughout college and graduate training. But as the need for the extra money became less and the demands on his time became more, logic pointed to an early retirement.

We were both very sad about his retirement at the time, as Ralph's musical career had been so much a part of our background together. I'll be the first to admit that in the past three years, we've tended to remember all the good times we had and conveniently forget all the negative aspects of it. But frankly, I've really missed Ralph's playing.

In the interim, of course, we've made good use of his musical equipment. When little Alan arrived, Ralph set up the microphone and amplifier next to the bassinet and wired them to a speaker on our bedside table so we could hear the baby at night. (Looked a little strange, admittedly. You sort of expected to see a billboard at the door proclaiming, "Live, nightly, from his crib . . . !") It also took a little while to adjust the system from PA to intercom. (The first time the baby cried, we practically got blasted out of bed.)

This past fall, however, I began to notice that Ralph's comments about going back into the music business were getting more frequent. I also began to find the classified section of the paper open to "musical instruments."

"Ralph," I said finally, "correct me if I'm wrong, but I think you are intending to buy something."

"Well," said Ralph, "I've been thinking of getting an electric piano to bring when there isn't a good piano available."

"Oh?" I said innocently. "Bring where?"

"To jobs with my new three-piece group, of course," said Ralph.

The plot thickened.

Now, most of the electric pianos of my experience had been fairly small, almost dainty-looking instruments. So imagine my surprise when I come home from my photography class one night and find this enormous object sitting in the middle of our bedroom.

"What is *that?*" I said.

"It's a Fender Rhodes," said Ralph happily.

"It looks more like the Colossus of," I said. "Is that thing really portable?"

"Sure," said Ralph, dismantling it into its component pieces. (The wonders of modern technology.)

The next morning Ralph was on the phone with his old contacts, hustling up some jobs, auditioning musicians, updating his music. There was a light back in Ralph's eyes that hadn't been there in a long time.

Looked like a good Christmas.

Appreciation

There's nothing worse than standing up for what you want only to find when you get it that you're not sure you want it.

Last summer, for example, I was having an appreciation crisis. As I'd often said to Ralph, I was willing to be somewhat oppressed, but I wanted him to appreciate me for it. But when you're oppressed and nobody even realizes you're oppressed, well, *that's* opression.

As I explained to Ralph, most of my feelings of unappreciation centered around household chores. Ralph, however, maintained that I wasn't appreciating all the things he did around the house either.

"Maybe we just ought to trade some chores for a while," said Ralph. "From now on, you mow the grass, water the lawn and the outside plants, and be the home handyman."

"All right," I said. "You're on."

"Good," said Ralph. "Before I forget, the bathroom tub and sink need caulking, and two electrical outlets in the living room need replacing before one of us gets fried plugging in the TV set."

"Before you get carried away," I said, "you'll be in charge of general cleaning, making the beds, food marketing, laundry, the inside plants, and feeding and watering the dog. That includes, by the way, putting in the dog's topknot in the morning."

"I *refuse* to do the dog's hair," said Ralph emphatically.

"I suppose you don't do windows either," I said. "It is not a matter of aesthetics, it's doctor's orders. The poor animal gets conjunctivitis when his hair hangs in his eyes."

"Of course," said Ralph, "you'll have to understand that by 'cleaning,' I'll be doing it by my standards instead of yours."

"Of course," I said. "But forget to make the beds and your lawn will be dead in a week."

"By the way," said Ralph, "we're out of fertilizer."

"That's OK," I said. "We're also out of food."

"While you're picking up the fertilizer," said Ralph, "get the lawn-mower blade sharpened. You'll also need to tune it. It's really past due."

"How do I do that?" I said uncertainly.

"It's a cinch," said Ralph. "Just throw in a new spark plug, adjust the timing, and lubricate the engine. An easy afternoon's work."

"This isn't fair," I said. "You're sticking me with an anemic lawn and a broken-down lawn mower."

"So you're sticking me with a house with no food and a dog with conjunctivitis."

"You know," I sighed, "I think the real issue here is that we don't want to do each other's chores so much as we want appreciation for the ones we already do."

"I think you're right," said Ralph. "And if you want to know the truth, I've really been appreciating you a lot in the past five minutes."

"Same here," I admitted.

"Frankly," said Ralph, "I really hate cleaning the house."

"Frankly," I said, "I really hate maintaining the yard."

"Gosh," said Ralph. "We're so compatible."

Epilogue

In the course of a marriage, there customarily occurs a continuing series of psychological divorces and remarriages as old, no-longer-working contracts — that is, spoken or unspoken arrangements between the partners — are replaced by those more compatible with the couple's current stage of growth. Issues that were prominent in the earlier years of the marriage frequently come to resolution in the second decade as both partners achieve greater confidence in themselves and their capabilities, come to accept and, indeed, integrate (rather than rebel against) the influence of their own parents, and are better able to tolerate some of the partner's less desirable qualities.

A successful marriage requires constant renegotiation and discussion of needs, and a continued confidence that each marital member could survive without the other.

It also requires putting up with a lot.

No more Cassie Milquetoast, me.

I stayed at my women's group until midnight one night last week and, on my way home, I singlehandedly, with no more protection than the strength of my frail body and a hatpin, stopped at Winchell's for a doughnut.

In case this doesn't sound particularly impressive, this was a remarkable feat, since after 10:00 P.M., everyone on the street looks like an ax murderer to me.

When you get engaged at nineteen and marry not long after, you miss a few things, like having your own apartment, staying out as late as you want, and risking your life at Winchell's. You never get to build up a certain confidence that you can survive on your own.

I first recognized the need to change several years ago when I began to realize that if Ralph died suddenly, I would have to be placed in a foster home. Oh, I changed fuses and dealt with household emergencies just fine. It was the idea of being responsible for myself that used to terrify me.

Certainly the first decade of our marriage has changed both Ralph and me. In the last ten years, we have endured five burglaries, the fire in which Ralph suffered second-degree burns, my mother's death, a cross-country move four days after Ralph ruptured his Achilles tendon playing tennis, two pituitary surgeries, a three-year wait for adoption, and a hold-up at gunpoint during a bank robbery.

As we reflected on this series of events during our tenth-anniversary dinner, we had to ask ourselves, "Had we known all this in advance, would either of us have shown up for the wedding?"

"That's a question?" said Ralph.

Of course, we've had many joys in that time too — friends we've made, kindnesses people have shown us, and most of all, Alan and Henri. So on the balance sheet, we're not doing too badly.

Even though we've survived our first ten years intact, I would have to question the wisdom of getting engaged at nineteen. My mother always said that women shouldn't get married until they're at least thirty, because they don't know who they are until then. At nineteen, I thought that was a lot of baloney because I already knew who I was. I was Ralph's girl friend.

I can't help but wonder at the grief we might have saved ourselves if both of us (but especially me) had waited a few more years before getting married. Frankly, I was not a particularly worldly person at nineteen. On our first date, I actually *believed* Ralph when he said he had a collection of rare tapestries in his room he wanted to show me. When we got up there, I didn't see anything that looked too rare or much like a tapestry, but was too polite to say anything.

Probably we married each other for all the wrong reasons. At the time, I was attracted to Ralph for his cool composure under pressure and his forcefulness, not to mention a myriad of other talents. He said he was initially attracted to me for my warmth and vulnerability. Describing those same characteristics at our second wedding anniversary, I think I called Ralph "cold and controlling" and he called me "neurotic." So much for the wisdom of mate selection.

I have also heard it said that if people stay married, it is for different reasons than they originally married one another for. This I would definitely say is true. Ralph and I have long agreed that he's had enough of my vulnerability and I've had enough of his forcefulness to last a lifetime.

In the last ten years, I think I've come a long way in taking control of my life. Ralph, for example, was so impressed that he has recently been asking me to handle some situations that require a really assertive person. (I should mention that he has also asked me to clean up some of the language that mysteriously appeared as Cassie Milquetoast's repressive facade started fading meekly into the woodwork.)

In the past few years, I have painfully conquered all sorts of territory — traveling by myself, making major decisions without Ralph, going to social events alone occasionally, making women friends more of a priority. Funny thing, I used to do all those things without a second thought before I got married.

So there I was at Winchell's last week, culminating several years of struggling for self-reliance. For the first time in a long while, I was out very late at night alone, no Ralph, no kids, no one to influence my choice of doughnut.

"I'll have a chocolate cruller," I said.

Not that I remember what it tasted like. I was too busy watching for the ax murderer.

When I was a kid, I always dreamed about growing up and having a house where all the plumbing worked at the same time. A home where no faucet went *plunk, plunk* through the night, where no buckets caught drips from leaky kitchen pipes, where showers drained all by themselves, and toilets could be flushed even in the spring.

Yes, this was my dream.

I guess every kid has things he doesn't like about the way his parents run their home, things he vows to do differently when he gets a place of his own. This, of course, is based on the child's uncanny ability to perceive that which he does not have. (Or in my case, that which he has but wishes he didn't.)

Now, Ralph and I both had wonderful parents with very levelheaded values who lived by the credo "Improvise!" (If there was less than a foot of water in the cellar, you didn't call the plumber.) They both made their homes more than comfortable, of course, but as Ralph put it, neither set of parents could be accused of being heavily into decorating. They much preferred to spend their money on vacations to the seashore and education for the children.

So, naturally, Ralph and I (totally unaware of the economic sacrifices that would be necessary) grew up craving House-Beautiful-and-Professionally-Repaired. A home where guests could use the facilities at will, without any prior instructions.

I remember very clearly a little talk Ralph and I had just before we were married.

"Louise," said Ralph at the time, "there is one thing that I could not tolerate your doing to me. You must never bring them into our home, and particularly not into our bedroom."

"You mean, other men?" I said incredulously.

"No," said Ralph. "Plastic flowers. Everything else is negotiable."

"OK, Ralph," I said, "I promise. But you promise me this. We will never live in a house with a septic tank, particularly not one at the bottom of a hill."

"All right," said Ralph, "if it means that much to you. Anything else you have feelings about?"

"I'd like white walls," I said. "No funny colors that are on sale. And no mixing dark and light woods in the same room."

"No slipcovers either," said Ralph. "No dish towels on doorknobs, or doilies on bureaus, or rugs over rugs."

"And no formica-topped anything," I said.

"No meals in the kitchen," said Ralph. "And we'll use the fireplace at will, even if it gets the house dirty."

"No mats over the rotten spots in the kitchen linoleum," I said.

"Our drinking glasses will match," added Ralph. "Nothing that ever held jelly will touch our lips. And we will water the lawn no matter what it costs."

Here it is ten years down the road already, and there are indeed no slipcovers on the furniture (which looks a little grungy), no plastic flowers (though we do have some dried), no doilies on bureaus or rugs over rugs (well, one rug over rug). We always eat in the dining alcove (there isn't any other place); the walls are white (mostly); and the woods match (in one room).

There is, however, a steady *plunk, plunk* in the background as the leak under the kitchen sink hits the bucket.

Well, you can't call the plumber for every little thing.

Ralph has a number of admirable qualities, mind you, but pushing in his sock drawer is not one of them.

Now, I suppose there are a lot of people who wonder what kind of a shrew would come down on a poor, hardworking guy about a lousy sock drawer. (Ralph is one of those people who wonders.)

To be honest, I'm still not sure why it is that we fight about the sock drawer, because the truth of it is, Ralph doesn't push in *any* of his drawers. (He's not too good on hanging up clothes either.) I guess the sock drawer is just sort of symbolic.

I think this is actually a pretty common problem. As the years have gone by, we've known a lot of other couples who have fights because one of them is neater than the husband.

If there's one thing I've learned, it's that this is not a problem you can effectively deal with until you understand its dynamics. This has taken me a long time.

For example, it was years before I figured out that Ralph actually prefers a clean and tidy house. (If you could see our bedroom, you'd understand why it took me years to figure it out.) Really, he does. But, as his bachelor sty so charmingly demonstrated, he will cheerfully live in utter squalor before he will tidy up anything himself.

Of course, a lot has to do with childhood training. Even more has to do with a lack of it. I don't think Ralph hung up his first shirt until he was twenty-three years old.

And I guess when it comes right down to it, I'll have to admit that the old neatness battle is an easy arena in which to fight out other conflicts of the marriage. This is a euphemistic way of saying that the number of shirts hanging from the curtain rod is sometimes directly proportional to how endearing I've made myself lately.

Actually, Ralph and I had it worked out reasonably well until about two years ago. (It's always been an issue, of course, but not always a major issue.) I realize now that this was because, up to that time, I had always worked *outside* the home.

"Ralph," I said one morning not too long ago, "you left all your drawers open again. As a matter of fact, our entire bedroom is a disaster."

"What's with the Mrs. Clean bit all of a sudden?" said Ralph. "Our bedroom doesn't look any different than it has ever looked."

"But I work at home now, Ralph," I said. "Our bedroom is also my office. I have to look at this junk all day."

"When we got married," Ralph pointed out, "you promised you weren't going to be the kind of wife who went berserk over a few flakes of dust."

"Who said anything about a few flakes of dust?" I said. "I'm talking about your wet towels on my typewriter."

"Oh," said Ralph apologetically, "sorry." He carefully picked up the soggy pile of towels from my desk and equally carefully moved it over to the bed.

There are some things in life you can't change.